Implementing Successful Wireless LANs

Implementing Successful Wireless LANs

Important Considerations in Deploying a Wireless Solution

Timothy M. Zimmerman

iUniverse, Inc.

New York Lincoln Shanghai

Implementing Successful Wireless LANs
Important Considerations in Deploying a Wireless Solution

iUniverse, Inc.

For information address:
iUniverse, Inc.
2021 Pine Lake Road, Suite 100
Lincoln, NE 68512
www.iuniverse.com

ISBN: 0-595-32875-X

Printed in the United States of America

With love and thanks to my wonderful wife, Trisha, along with our two daughters, Jillian and Kaylin, for their patience and encouragement.

ABOUT THE AUTHOR

Tim Zimmerman has more than a decade of experience in local area wireless data communications, contributing to the international wireless community as an author and speaker. He's served in marketing, product management and executive capacities at various wireless and advanced technology companies. He has contributed to the industry as part of the IEEE 802.11 working group and as part of the founding team for WLANA (Wireless LAN Alliance) and WLIF (Wireless LAN Interoperability Forum). He has undergraduate degrees in physics and computer science from Cornell College in Mt. Vernon, IA and a master's degree in business administration from the University of Iowa. Tim, his wife, Trisha and their two daughters reside in Charlotte, NC.

CONTENTS

PREFACE

Like the axiom, "The only thing constant is change," doing business in our global economy continues to change as companies grow, expand, reorganize, relocate and downsize every day. Each new step introduces variables into the business equation, and with each new variable is the need for more information.

In the past, people collected or exchanged business critical data using paper-based systems. But as technology has advanced, so have the methods of collecting, moving and processing the data. Additionally, people today are no longer bound to their desks; they have become more mobile, moving throughout office, factory and warehouse or distribution facility in search of "real time" data to run the business better and faster. In the rush to have it "now," businesses also need "more" of elusive data needed to run the business. The methodology for providing this information has progressed from yesterday's archaic paper-based processes entered by clerks into mainframes to today's laptops running enterprise resource planning (ERP) applications that have collected data via mobile workers using traditional keyboard entry and expanding to other technologies such as speech recognition, RFID or bar code scanning technologies. In the midst of the information explosion, it is an impossible task for IT managers to run wires to provide communications to every possible location where data is collected. Therefore, wireless communication has emerged as the next evolutionary step to provide a complete customer solution—extending the wired LAN to the mobile front line worker.

Because the 1970's, wireless LAN (WLAN) technologies have slowly evolved as a viable alternative to, and extension of, wired LANs. Designed to address the various issues associated with placing technology in the hands of mobile workers, wireless solutions took the "green screen," or the desktop computer, and allowed anyone to enter or use data available on any server in the enterprise at any time. In the early adoption stages of market development, the technology was new but radio frequency data collection (RFDC) solutions proliferated warehousing and retail vertical markets because the return on investment in these applications (such as shipping and receiving) was typically six months to one year.

As solutions were successfully deployed, customers became more comfortable with wireless technology and the benefits it could provide. Customers in vertical markets who were targeted by wireless solution providers began to expand their use of wireless technology to other applications, such as quality control applications, that use quantitative data collection including bar code scanning, keyboard entry or speech recognition for hands- and eyes-free operations. Today's products combine different technologies to further expand the functionality of portable devices. Over time, markets such as the retail industry have used wireless mobile computing for a variety of applications, such as price verification and changes as well as floor inventory checking. The newest and fastest growing vertical market segment involves the use of WLANs in healthcare applications, where nurses are using wireless to provide inventory management for hospital equipment or to collect vital patient information.

Vertical markets with specific solutions have continued to provide the most substantial and quickest benefits. But slowly, horizontal markets are emerging and solutions are moving to the carpeted office spaces, schools and even our homes. Instead of running Ethernet cable, we are expanding the reach of computers to touch the infrastructure using wireless PC cards or wireless enabled laptops. Instead of running wires through the walls of buildings, wireless has become an easy way to communicate between disparate computer platforms. IEEE 802.11 working groups have continued to provide a platform that allows the functionality to expand. And by providing a standard, the ability exists for competition to facilitate cost reduction. The original IEEE 802.11 working group provided a 2 Megabyte standard that was extended to 11 Mbps by the IEEE 802.11b standard, and the 802.11g provides over 54 Mbps. Working groups continue to expand the performance envelope.

As more people use wireless technology to solve their problems with an attractive return on investment, the number and types of applications continue to grow. According to one study, the average time to fully pay back the initial costs of installation is less than nine months. Ninety-seven percent of customers said that wireless technology exceeded their expectations, with over ninety percent reporting plans to continue to deploy additional applications using wireless. As with most technologies, the road has not been easy, and the face of wireless technology has changed from the original installations. Initial solutions in the 1970's were deployed using narrow band radios with hub and spoke architectures. Today, Ethernet-based spread spectrum solutions operate over 1,000 times faster, and technology is continuing to advance the capabilities and capacity to meet the needs of new markets and expanding applications. We will see the continued success of solutions in vertical markets and the emergence of horizontal applications, which will add to the fuel of the overall market's growth. Many of these horizontal applications are associated with access to the Internet and intranet in the office and at home. As the diversity of applications emerges, wireless solutions must have the flexibility to allow customers to deploy today's solution and migrate to tomorrow's technology as their needs evolve.

The goal of this book is to unveil the magic associated with implementing this unexplained new technology. It will review and explain the issues that surround wireless in-premise communication—as a technology, as a wireless system, and as it is integrated into the enterprise infrastructure.

Overview of the Markets and Applications

In most corporate boardrooms, IT managers are raising the question of how they should deploy wireless within their business. Every analyst agrees that the potential market will be huge as applications continue to expand. The problem is that the technology for wireless is continually being improved, and vendors are constantly addressing new issues such as needs for higher speeds, security or network management. Additionally, a wireless solution isn't as easy to understand as its wired communication counterparts. This purported extension to the wired LAN has a new set of rules and a new set of issues that need to be resolved. There is also a choice of wireless technologies—such as 802.11b/g, Bluetooth, or 802.11a. Lurking in the corners are many IT managers who have older, vendor-specific, application-oriented, proprietary wireless data collection solutions installed, which independently try to resolve data collection issues in a variety of different transmission frequencies—including 400-450 KHz (UHF) or spread spectrum solutions in the 900 MHz or 2.4 GHz frequencies. Choosing and integrating the right wireless technology and/or maintaining an existing solution is one of the most important issues facing IT managers planning on extending their infrastructures using wireless communications. What complicates matters about wireless is the lack of consistent information about the older technology and integration issues beyond installing the access points. In many cases, manufacturers are too busy emphasizing the bits and bytes or speeds and feeds of the radio technology and forgetting the business application and the integration of wireless communication into the corporate enterprise. The key is to remember the business problem that is being solved. Wireless *can* be cost effective, but you can make it effective only if you really understand it.

As a business implementer, you need only to follow several basic tenets as you look to deploy a wireless solution. First, you must understand that no single wireless standard or technology will solve all of your problems. Any serious corporate wireless strategist needs to fully define the problem(s) you are trying to solve, and then include the different products that provide the best solution(s). Problems can arise when people try to force-fit one technology into an application for which it was not meant. Secondly, wireless itself should not

1

warrant a business decision. Wireless is only the technology. It is important to comprehend that different technologies are introduced into the market to solve different problems. Different commercial pressures will dictate which is the correct approach, and with the right knowledge the best decision can be made for the problem you are solving.

Benefits of Wireless Applications

The benefits that wireless brings as part of a business solution can depend on the implementation. Common benefits include mobility, real time access to information, the ability to reach areas that cannot be wired and the realization of a return on the investment.

MOBILITY OR PORTABILITY

Mobility or portability is the freedom to move around and not be tied to a desk or workstation. When we look at our environment, we see that many of our tasks require us to gather information from multiple places, whether it is counting inventory, checking prices, entering the vehicle identification number from a newly built automobile, downloading class notes or accessing email from a hotel room or an airport hot spot. Instead of reading information and running back to a computer that is tethered to a wired network, wireless communication gives us the capability to complete the same task, eliminating the need to write the information down or to try remembering it as we return to the computer. Mobility gives wireless users the flexibility and benefit of taking the equipment to the data. It also makes entering the information more accurate because it is entered only once. At the same time, it eliminates the delay from gathering the information and entering it, and gives businesses real time access to the information.

REAL TIME UPDATES AND ACCESS

Many of the operations that are being wirelessly enabled have historically been completed using pencil and paper. In the past, once the work was completed, the paper was collected and then sent to a data processing clerk who would type the information into a computer. Trying to read someone else's handwriting was among the problems that could cause several-days delay from collection to input. Whether the information was for a database, warehouse management system, tracking system, payroll system or one of many other programs, it was used to run the daily operations of businesses. Faster input of the data allows for reporting to be completed in real time instead of in a batch mode or on the next day. The inability to get the information into the system can delay decisions that are necessary to the success of businesses. Conversely, information also needs to be able to get out of the system. Wireless communication allows real time access to information, again allowing decisions to be made more quickly.

DIFFICULT TO WIRE AREAS

Often there are obstacles that require the use of technology as a solution. Situations exist where traditional network solutions to distribute or gather information cannot be used because there is difficulty in installing the necessary wired infrastructure. For example, older buildings of major cities such as Boston, Philadelphia and New York City are being classified as historic while they continue to serve as places of business. This means that running a new network connection through the wall, while feasible, may require approval that could cause significant delays or may not be approved at all. Attaching an access point to an existing network connection or to a computer allows the network to be extended to the users. Another issue that exists with older buildings could be the presence of asbestos or other substances. This would prevent wiring the building without incurring significant remodeling/reconstruction costs. Implementation of a wireless network eliminates the need to do any wiring while gaining the benefit of communication.

COST SAVINGS

The biggest reason for any technology explosion is the cost saving benefit and the ability to realize a return on investment. There are several factors that can be used when a wireless infrastructure needs to be cost-justified: reducing redundancy, improving productivity, recabling/relocation cost, temporary location capabilities and growing markets and applications. These factors can provide a cost savings when the company is expanding or a productivity benefit for existing operations.

Reducing Redundancy

In many of the vertical markets, wireless is used for data collection applications. This solution eliminates the need for information to be written down on a piece of paper and then given to someone who enters the information into a computer. The wireless handheld data collection industry has provided cost savings and return on investment by allowing information to be entered by the worker. This methodology streamlines operations and provides savings.

Improving Productivity

Reducing redundancy and improving productivity usually go hand in hand when wireless is deployed, especially for data collection applications. While the elimination of writing data down on a piece of paper may be attributed to the implementation of bar codes or other automated data collection capability, the elimination of these extra steps is due to wireless communication. Wireless can also improve productivity by allowing work to be completed on a timely basis, such as having wireless in classrooms, conference rooms, airports, hotel rooms or "hot spots" that allow enterprise connectivity. Wireless "hot spots" are areas where access points are placed in public places, such as airports or hotel lobbies, allowing personal data assistants (PDAs) or laptop computers to access wired resources (such as the Internet) for free or for a small fee.

Cost of Recabling/Relocation

Whether businesses are growing or contracting, people are constantly being moved to better use the available space, perhaps for departmental or project reasons. By using wireless connections for laptop or workstation access to the enterprise infrastructure, there is no need to rewire for the changes. The savings in construction and labor easily provides the necessary return on investment.

Creating Temporary Locations

Businesses also have a need for temporary enterprise connections such as training classes, projects, meetings or virtual office where personnel are away from their home offices or other working locations. Connecting via wireless is a natural choice, eliminating the need for any wired solution, whether the communication is an ad hoc network or one that extends the wired infrastructure to the workers. Consulting companies that audit corporate accounting, assist in installing manufacturing systems or assist in management restructuring need to consolidate information for reporting purposes. In the past, this may have been done via a "sneakernet," in which diskettes or FLASH cards provided section updates to a report. A wireless ad hoc network makes this type of communication so much easier.

Markets and Applications

The supply chain for companies has traditionally been a rich vein of opportunity for wireless communications as businesses recognize the need for real time updates and realize quick returns for their investment. As vertical markets experienced success in using wireless communications to extend the reach of the workers to the point of information, they began using wireless for applications that required mobility and finally to cover the last mile to where work needed to be completed. For example, operations in the supply chain, such as distribution, deployed wireless in the distribution centers to achieve accuracy and productivity improvements, and then into transportation to keep track of the inventory as it was moved. Next, wireless moved into the retail store for management applications, and finally into the home for ordering products.

Wireless solutions then moved into broad-based horizontal markets such as offices, healthcare and hospitality, allowing everyone to work more efficiently. From the warehouse to the office or from the school to the home, people began taking wireless everywhere.

WAREHOUSING AND DISTRIBUTION

The ability to allow data to be collected using mobile workers throughout a warehouse or distribution center of any size is extremely attractive. In the past, information about their work had been based on paper forms. Whether it was a pick list, receiving manifest or shipping document, batches of forms, or "tickets," were preprinted based on the information that was available at the end of the previous day. These tickets might have been the manifests for scheduled deliveries or printouts of work that needed to be completed for the day, such as picking orders or moving products that had been entered into the warehouse management software (WMS), enterprise resource planning (ERP) software or transferred to a vendor via electronic document interchange (EDI). Supervisors typically assigned the tasks to employees. Once the work was completed, these forms were collected and input into the computer system or mainframe so that business decisions could be made, based on that data, for the next day.

When paper and pencil methods are used, often the delay from collection to input is 24 hours or more. The return on investment for a business moving from paper-based operations to wireless data collection is very quick, as it eliminates paperwork, reduces errors, increases productivity and provides the business with real time information.

The basic operations of warehousing and/or distribution are receiving, put away, picking, cycle counting/inventory and shipping benefit from wireless data collection. There are a variety of different methodologies such as bar code, keyboard, speech recognition that are used to collect the data and transfer it over a wireless network to accomplish these basic business operations, which may vary by industry or implementer. Depending on the market segment each solution realizes the increase in the productivity and accuracy of the operations.

Receiving Goods

When products are received at the dock, it is important to understand which product has arrived and the quantities that can now be used by the business. In the past, a receiving manifest was printed and workers unloaded products and checked off the received product with the types and amounts on the preprinted manifest. It took time to receive the products and get the information entered into an inventory system. Lost time and productivity spent correcting the errors in reading handwriting or miskeyed data provided the return on investment needed for wireless data collection.

Wireless handhelds replace the paper manifest at the dock. Using wireless, workers enter the information into the handheld data collection computer where it wirelessly updates the warehouse management system (WMS) or enterprise resource planning (ERP) system. In addition, to eliminate a redundant level of inputting the information, it also eliminates the day that it takes to be able to use the information. Received products are immediately known to the WMS and can be used to complete orders for the product.

Put Away and Picking Goods

Once the product is received, it can be delivered to a warehouse location. Another return on investment opportunity is reducing the number of products that are lost because they were put away in the wrong location, perhaps because the location was full and an alternative location was needed or they need to immediately be moved to another dock door for shipping. Wirelessly enabling workers in the warehouse or distribution center for put away and picking operations allows businesses to address exceptions such as damaged product or empty location, in addition to entering the basic information about picking or put away. The cost of an inaccurate order increases as it leaves the warehouse, because the mispicked item cannot be used for other orders and the transportation costs associated with getting the first item back into inventory and sending the second item add up. The Warehouse Education Resource Council (WERC) reports that companies average 90-95 percent accuracy in order picking. This means that one in ten or one in twenty items picked incurs that expense of correcting the problem. One of the big issues with wireless data collection for picking was that picking some products is a hands- and eyes-free operation. With the introduction of speech recognition as an input method that works in conjunction with scanning and keyboard entry over the wireless infrastructure, workers can now achieve the productivity that could not be matched by pick to label or pick to light systems.

Freezers

Whether it is a freezer or a cooler, writing down information is difficult when you are trying to do it while wearing gloves (or trying to take them off to write and then putting them on again). Freezers can be a harsh environment, yet meat, cheese, dairy, ice cream and other frozen foods still need to be picked and inventoried just like other products in the supply chain. Additionally, meat and cheese need more information, such as weights and date codes, for product tracking. While wireless communication remains the foundation of this solution, speech recognition now solves the data collection problems of frost on labels or punching keys with gloves. The key is taking the data collection to the point of where the information is to provide productivity and accuracy.

Shipping Goods

Shipping moves products out of the warehouse as the orders are fulfilled. Wireless handhelds can provide the extra functionality of auditing the order and/or shipping the products out of the warehouse. Once the information has been entered and the shipping function completed, the order can be invoiced. Wireless modules added to network printers allow documents to be printed immediately at the dock door once the pallet consolidation or shipping information is complete, thus eliminating another step and adding to supply chain productivity.

Cross docking

Cross docking is a hybrid operation of moving goods from receiving to shipping without storing them in a warehouse. Real time access for goods that have landed on the receiving dock allows the warehouse management system to identify orders for that product that need to be shipped immediately. Moving the goods from the receiving dock to the shipping dock eliminates several steps, such as putting the product in a location and retrieving it, therefore increasing productivity.

Cross Docking Creates a Virtual Distribution Center

With proper planning, some companies can make cross docking the standard process in their just-in-time operation. An example company makes daily deliveries to stores along routes. Orders for additional products are placed directly to the vendor with an update to the distribution center. Vendors arrive each day with the ordered products that were scheduled for delivery to an empty distribution facility. The products are received using wireless handhelds, then distributed with the same handhelds to the various routes, in a preput stage, and then to each store. By the end of the day, trucks are loaded with the goods—using wireless handhelds with an invoice from a wireless enabled printer. Products are delivered to the stores with the handheld doing batch data collection. Once the wireless handheld is within range of the enterprise infrastructure and communication is established, the collected information is uploaded. The productivity improvements of wireless allow the warehouse facility to start and end each day empty, while being able to record all product that is received and distributed to the local locations.

Manufacturing Products

Many of the operations from warehousing and distribution are similar to those in manufacturing, as components are received and stocked for later use. Picked items are delivered internally to locations and used in the manufacturing process. In addition to data collection, new operations include asset management, work-in-process tracking, process monitoring and time and attendance. Wireless data collection allows cable runs to be eliminated for test equipment, printers, programmable logic units (PLU) and other equipment on the manufacturing line. Equipment tags allow expensive inventory, such as engine blocks in automotive manufacturing, to be tracked while being built.

Transportation

Keeping track of inventory extends beyond the four walls of warehouses and distribution centers. Wireless communication is often used for yard management (the process of keeping track of trucks that are waiting to be received). Upon entering the delivery gate, the truck is assigned a location on the lot. It is retrieved and moved to a dock door by a handler who is using wireless to get the correct lot location and dock location. Rail yards and shipping ports worldwide use wireless for container inventory. Containers are placed in storage locations that have grid identifiers at the dock or the yard. This application is a good example of how UHF technology continues to solve business problems. With its 1 million square foot plus coverage capability, the small communication pipe is able to satisfy the application needs. While a standards based 2.4 GHz solution could also provide a solution, it would take many more access points, as well as power and cable runs to support these multi-acre facilities.

In Store Retail

Retail organizations are constantly ordering products, changing prices, selling products to consumers and keeping track of all aspects of the transaction. Product movement through retail stores is almost a science, as the retail industry continues to be an early adopter of wireless technology and its productivity applications. A wireless infrastructure enables clerks and store personnel to perform their functions while on the store floor. Price checking and changes or inventory updates can be made on the floor with the information updated automatically in the store inventory database. Up-to-date information allows store management to make staffing and other management decisions while on the floor working with the retail team. With the advent of 11 Mbps wireless connectivity, retailers are also losing the cables on point of sale registers and information kiosks, so that they can be placed closer to the customer or outside for sales events.

HEALTHCARE

In hospitals and other healthcare facilities, access to information can be a matter of life and death. Wireless connectivity allows doctors and nurses to leverage information at the bedside or "point of care" to make decisions.

In the past, doctors kept charts on patients as they made their rounds, visiting each patient. One problem with this procedure was that doctors visited multiple patients during their rounds, and directions they gave for the first patient needed to wait until the chart was returned and transcribed before anyone could take action. Wireless eliminates the wait by allowing doctors to immediately update records. This same update capability applies to nurses as they check and input patient vital signs such as blood pressure, pulse and temperature.

Wireless also benefits auxiliary services such as oxygen or medication delivery, so that information is available when services are performed. Again, the availability of information (such as when medication was given) can be very important to assuring a successful recovery.

HOSPITALITY

The hospitality industry ranks with warehouse and distribution as an early adopter of wireless communications. In the mid-1980's, hospitality companies were putting wireless handhelds in the hands of waitstaff. Imagine lying on the beach at a resort when a server asks if you would like a drink. The server enters your order into a wireless handheld, and the order automatically prints at the bar. A runner brings the drink, which has already been charged to your room, immediately, instead of you waiting for the waitress to walk the order back and bring it later. The same scenario works in a capacity crowd at a ball game. Instead of waiting in line, your order is taken at your seat and charged to your credit card without missing a second of the game. Finally, quality restaurants use wireless to have your soup or salad out to the table before the waitress finishes taking your order.

The use of wireless communications has expanded in the hospitality industry in an effort to provide better service to customers. Now, in addition taking orders, rental car companies use wireless to check in drivers at their cars when returning the vehicles. Ski resorts use wireless for lift ticket verification, which gives them information on who is using what ski run as well as whether the ticket is valid for the day. Major golf tournaments use wireless to input the results of players as they complete each hole. Again, the implementation can vary; some solutions have an input device at each hole to record everyone who completes that hole, while others assign an input device with an operator who travels with each pair of golfers as they traverse the golf course, entering the information as they complete each hole.

OFFICE

Extending wireless connectivity to the carpeted office area was a natural next step for companies in vertical markets that were deploying wireless in warehouse and distribution centers. These early adopters recognized the benefits of wireless, and as they became comfortable with the technology they began solving other business problems. The smaller form factor of a PC card or turning on integrated wireless capabilities and the decreased cost also accelerated the use of wireless, but the return on investment was difficult unless reorganization, restructuring, growth or downsizing mandated a change in the facility, requiring cables and power to rerun.

While wireless extended the wired Ethernet for temporary workgroups, conference rooms and ad hoc teams to share information, one of the biggest benefits was for employees, such as sales personnel, who visited the corporate office for a few days to a week but were not permanent (or vice versa—management visiting remote offices). Rather than having to locate an Ethernet connection, visiting employees were handed a PC card that used a preset profile. They were then connected through a Virtual Private Network (VPN) to the network resources needed to access email and print. This flexibility assured that the IT team did not have to make sure that there was a bank of RJ45 connectors installed throughout the building to accommodate visiting employees. Once the access point infrastructure was installed, other applications could be implemented. Printers were no longer attached to a specific location; they could be moved closer to the people using them within a department who needed temporary high priority, such as to print projects or customer proposals.

EDUCATION

Educational institutions have found that wireless connectivity provides students with universal 24-hour access to campus services so that they can sign up for classes, download and upload assignments, access campus libraries, collaborate on study projects, contact professors and conduct research, as well as connect to the Internet from anywhere on campus. School implementation of wireless varies, as some provide access in hot spots such as classrooms, libraries and dorm rooms while others provide ubiquitous coverage throughout the campus, including outside, so that connections can be established and maintained as students travel from one building to another.

OTHER USES

The ideas are endless as consumers get comfortable with the technology and continue to think of new ways to use it.

Hazardous Areas

Buildings containing hazardous materials, such as asbestos, in the ceiling and walls often cannot be wired with Ethernet cabling. Wireless provides communications connectivity without disturbing the hazardous material. While the local building or health codes will require that the offending material be removed, this is usually an extremely expensive and time-consuming task.

Other hazardous material areas include paint rooms, where the products may be stored or mixed, or other chemical areas. These areas in manufacturing and warehouse facilities are separated from other open-air parts of the facility, yet wireless can be used to provide inventory control or information (such as mixing instructions) to people who work in these areas.

Sealed Areas

The uses of wireless technology continue to expand and reach to areas where typical cables sometimes cannot go, such as sealed rooms. For example, "clean rooms" used for research or rooms for certain production processes, such as microchip manufacturing, must be sealed to prevent dust or other contaminants from entering. This means that the places where wire is typically run like conduits do not exist in these areas without special protection. For this situation, wireless is an excellent connectivity tool that provides a link to the network through the glass and walls—without breaking the seal of the room.

Ad hoc for disasters

At the point of a disaster (such as a plane crash, train wreck, hurricane, tornado or earthquake), wireless can be used to set up a temporary ad hoc network between individuals or agencies to gather, log and exchange information.

Ad hoc for military uses

Moving all the time over a variety of terrain, wireless communication allows data and other information to be exchanged. The short range of wireless makes it ideal for high-speed communications for a network of people who need constant communications. For the technology warrior, this data may also be video, speech, biometric or other.

WLAN Regulations, Standards and Organizations

Overview

Rules and regulations govern all aspects of our lives; wireless is no different. With most of the publicity focused on IEEE 802 and the standards efforts, one might assume that the regulations for wireless are ubiquitous. They are not; there are different regulations, depending on the frequency being used and the country that is using it. Until wireless gained popularity in industrial, home and office applications, the market weaved through the complexity of delivering wireless solutions to the global economy. In the beginning, wireless solutions operated in the 450-470 MHz ultra-high frequency (UHF) radio band for commercial applications. Applications were limited to the amount of data that could be transferred because initial solutions were limited to 1200 baud. A brief comparison shows how far wireless technology has come over the years as 2.4 GHz IEEE 802.11g radios have a throughput capacity of 54 Mbps, which is over 50,000 times faster than the original UHF radios. Deploying a wireless solution was not as easy as it is today. In the United States, UHF solutions were regulated by the FCC and required licenses for specific frequencies. Equipment could not be ordered for customers until the license was approved, and because the radio crystals were embedded into components, some companies applied for multiple licenses to be available throughout the United States to give them flexibility. This upfront planning not only assisted in a quicker license, but also in service spares for equipment.

In 1985, the FCC announced the availability of the Industrial, Scientific and Medical (ISM) band. This was a band of frequencies that could be used by coexisting wireless solutions. The immediate major benefits of the ISM band were that it is license free, does not require filing for frequency allocation with the FCC and it is capable of supporting higher data rate wireless communications than the current 9600-baud UHF solutions in the market. The ISM bands are located at 900 MHz, 2,4 GHz, and 5.7 GHz and vary in width from

26 MHz to 150 MHz. In 1997, the FCC also provided three Unlicensed National Information Infrastructure (UNII) bands in the 5 GHz range.

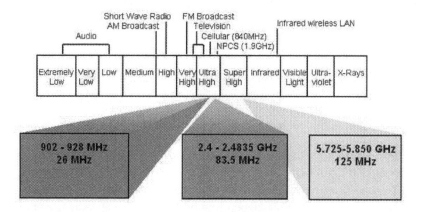

The introduction of the ISM band in 1985 coincided with the explosion of wired networking. While the move for early adopters of wireless technology across the chasm was quick because of the rapid return on investment, it was further accelerated by improvements in wired networking. Ethernet was clearly a catalyst that has continued the growth in the wireless market. Ethernet provided a uniform wired infrastructure for all wireless access points and quickly adopted the physical media changes as Ethernet moved from 10Base5 to 10Base2 to 10BaseT connections.

Because the late 1980's, the innovations and improvements in wireless LANs have tracked closely and utilized many of the changes in the wired world, both from a technology standpoint (such as medium detection) as well as from a system implementation standpoint, addressing security and device management. While the market continues to grow, it is important to understand the different types of wireless that are being used and how the implementations may differ worldwide.

Governing Agencies for Wireless

While the need for wireless is universal, the agencies governing wireless communication from one country to another differ. This has been part of the difficulty in creating a worldwide wireless standard and driving its continued growth. The Federal Communications Commission (FCC) governs the use of radio frequency in the United States. Others include the following:

- ➤ Department of Communication (DOC)—Canada
- ➤ European Telecommunication Standards Institute (ETSI)—European Community, Switzerland, Norway, Iceland and Liechtenstein
- ➤ Ministry of Public Management, Home Affairs, Posts and Telecommunications—Japan

These agencies cover the implementation of wireless whether it is a licensed frequency (such as UHF in the US) or unlicensed in the ISM and U-NII bands.

FEDERAL COMMUNICATION COMMISSION

The FCC is an independent government agency that reports directly to Congress (www.fcc.gov). The FCC was established by the Communications Act of 1934 and is charged with regulating interstate and international communications by radio, television, wire, satellite and cable. The FCC's jurisdiction covers not only the continental US, but all 50 states and US possessions such as Puerto Rico, Guam and The Virgin Islands. Many Central and South American countries also accept FCC certification for operation of equipment in their countries.

DEPARTMENT OF CANADA

The Department of Canada (DOC) devices must meet all Class B requirements of the Canadian Interference-Causing Equipment Regulations and be certified to RSS-139-1 and RSS-210 for 2.4 GHz spread spectrum devices. The use of the device either partially or completely outdoors may require the user to obtain a license for the system, according to Canadian regulations.

EUROPEAN TELECOMMUNICATION STANDARDS INSTITUTE

The European Telecommunications Standards Institute (ETSI) is a not-for-profit organization whose mission is to produce the telecommunications standards. All WLAN equipment used in the 2.4 GHz band must comply with the European Commission's Radio and Telecommunications Terminal Equipment Directive, 1999/5/EC (R&TTE) governing radio equipment self-certification and conformity in accordance with the applicable standards (ETS 300-328) for wireless LANs.

National regulators are responsible for controlling the use of the 2.4 GHz band in their respective countries. As a result, regulations can vary across different European countries, with dramatic results on the development of the WLAN marketplace.

France imposes severe restrictions on the amount of frequency available for WLAN operations. In France, only part of the 2.4 GHz ISM band can be used. The frequency range 2.4465 GHz to 2.4835 GHz is available. In addition, some applications require authorization from the Ministry of Defense. The frequency restriction is typically handled by vendors in setting up the drivers for the radio, but still uses the radio that is used worldwide.

Ministry of Public Management, Home Affairs, Posts and Telecommunications

The Association of Radio Industries and Businesses (ARIB) was chartered by the Minister of Public Management, Home Affairs, Posts and Telecommunications (MPHPT) as a public service corporation on May 15, 1995. The MPMHPT designated ARIB as "the Center for Promotion of Efficient Use of Radio Spectrum" and "the Designated Frequency Change Support Agency under the provisions of the Radio Law." Under the designation, it conducts studies and Research & Development, provides consultation services for radio spectrum coordination in Japan, and cooperates with other organizations around the world.

Licensed Radio Frequency Bands

Licensed radio bands were the first wireless implementations, and they continue to be used for special purpose applications. In the United States, they are defined as 430-470 MHz or UHF (Ultra High Frequency). Other countries also use this band for wireless communication, but the rules of operation may vary. Regulations in Europe and Japan make it difficult to deploy wireless in the UHF band but the benefits continue to outweigh the complex commercial solutions. One of most popular applications for the UHF band has been for licensed voice communication such as "walkie-talkies." This band was initially governed by FCC Part 90 in the United States and has been redefined by FCC Part 88. The Part 88 changes made the channel spacing smaller, which required all existing implementations to either be upgraded to the new Part 88 radios or to spread spectrum technology. This technology is frequently referred to as "narrow band" radio because the throughput is small, though the coverage area is very large.

UHF WIRELESS INNOVATIONS

With the smaller data pipe, vendors made many innovations, such as screen mapping, and modified protocols in order to meet the customer application needs. The primary application for UHF was data input as mobile clients emulated the protocol of fixed terminals attached to mainframes.

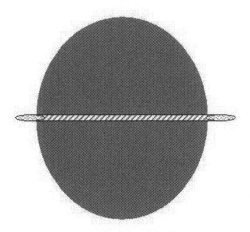

Handling Large Screens of Information

The IBM and DEC mainframe screens that mobile handhelds emulated consisted of 2,000 characters (80 columns by 25 lines). Sending each character presented two problems: firstly, that sending all 2,000 characters used valuable bandwidth and secondly, that the smaller display on the mobile handheld could not display the entire screen. Software companies presented many different products, including the following:

➢   A virtual screen by some vendors allowed the user to page up and down, or arrow right and left, to see the entire contents of the mainframe screen.

➢   A software middleware package remapped the mainframe screen or multiple screens to the mobile handheld using only the fields that were needed or that required input. Additional functionality could also be added by the middleware, which could process the input data before sending it to the mainframe application. These products continue to be used by the marketplace for IBM AS/400 and ES/400 solutions, where the customer does not have source code for the host application.

> ➤ A mirroring software option by some vendors included screens that were remapped for the new display size of the mobile client. The new screens also were cached on the mobile handheld, so that only an identifier was sent to the handheld over the small UHF pipe for a new screen to be displayed, and only the data was sent back for processing and integration into the host application.

Wireless Optimized Protocols

Because there was no interoperability with UHF wireless solutions and TCP/IP was not used because of the overhead associated with packets of information, each vendor had its own protocol for identifying which handheld the message was going to, as well as roaming and other system messages. These protocols optimized the header and the size of the packet to assure quick delivery and fast response over the available bandwidth. While TCP/IP has become the most common protocol for wireless (following in the footsteps of wired communications) now that the bandwidth can support the increased overhead, these wireless optimized protocols are still coexist today for some terminal emulation implementations. These optimized protocols have lost favor over the years, mainly because they are not recognized by other wired appliances (such as routers) and because the non-routable required that all network segments that used wireless be bridged together. These non-routable proprietary packets also show up as foreign packets, which causes alerts for many network management software packages (especially with the increased importance of network security).

Special Terminal Emulation Packages

The functionality of terminal emulation also changed. For many vertical market solutions, the host application ran on an IBM AS/400, ES/9000 (before IBM renamed them) or DEC or UNIX platform. For AS/400s, mobile handhelds emulated IBM 5250 displays. Customers with System/36 or ES/9000 mainframes had mobile handhelds that emulated IBM 3270 displays that ran on a SNA/SDLC infrastructure. VT100, VT220 and VT340 were part of the ANSI specifications that were used for DEC or UNIX host platforms. These specifications were written with large desktop display in mind, not a mobile handheld. Therefore, changes were made to accommodate extra functionality. Unfortunately, these changes were vendor-specific, but included functionality required for scanning bar codes instead of manually entering data. Some fields had a preamble that identified whether the information was keyed in on a keyboard or scanned, which was used for log in verification. Others translated information into known formats. For example, "Auto scan enter" was translated to "Auto enter," where the enter key was automatically pressed once the field was full, or in this case, once there was a good scan.

Over time, companies reverse-engineered competitive special features so that they could operate with applications where the special characters were used.

Moving Forward

While many of the features that were developed for UHF applications exist today with spread spectrum solutions, today UHF solutions are limited to special purpose applications. Because UHF solutions continue to be vendor-specific, the return on investment is the driver for choosing this over standards-based solutions. Customers who select UHF typically have two requirements. Firstly, they may have a very large facility that needs many acres of coverage (such as shipping port or a rail yard). Secondly, the amount of information being transferred cannot be too small because the UHF offers speeds only up to 19.2 kbps, which comparably is slower than most dial-up modem connections.

Unlicensed Radio Frequency Bands

In 1985, the FCC authorized the use of spread spectrum radio technology in the 902-928 MHz 2.4-2.4835 GHz and 5.725-5.850 GHz frequency bands. FCC Part 15 rules allow unlicensed use of spread spectrum data communications in these bands. These bands are commonly referred to as 900 MHz, 2.4 GHz and 5.7 GHz, respectively. Spread spectrum wireless networking, like many other technologies, came of age under the guidance of the military. The military needed a simple, easily implemented and secure method of exchanging data in a combat environment.

900 MHz

In the US, the 902-928 MHz band was the first band to be used by wireless communication vendors for vertical data collection applications. While the physical radio layer was in the spread spectrum band, the wireless protocols continued were, and are, proprietary, so there was no interoperability. Additionally, because it is spread spectrum, the band was open to everyone. As a result it attracted cordless telephones, devices to extend in-home TV signals and vehicle locating systems. This band is used only in the US, Canada and a few other countries, such as Brazil. Part of the band 915-928 MHz can be found in Australia and New Zealand. The band has limited use because it was already allocated in other countries. For example, it is not permitted in Europe because this part of the frequency band is allocated for emergency services.

The 900 MHz band was the first ISM to be used for wireless communications, but there were no standards for use even though the IEEE 802.11 committee was first convened to create a standard using 900 MHz. With the growth of personal computers in the early 1990's, companies such as Proxim and Aironet introduced products that were not specifically integrated into a device. These ISA card radios could be installed into personal computers for wireless communication to access points for the office market. In general, 900 MHz solution had the following functionality:

> Two spread spectrum modulations, frequency hopping and direct sequence, were allowed and implemented.

> Some companies broke the band into three or more sub-bands.

> Speeds were also very different, from 60 Kbps to over 300 Kbps.

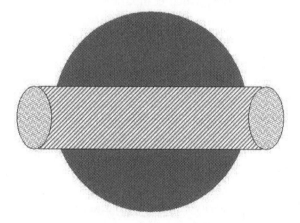

Many 900 MHz solutions still exist because they provide excellent coverage. Customers are also seeking many of the features of today's wireless implementations, such as Ethernet connectivity. The customer is not necessarily looking for multiple vendor interoperability. For IT managers with applications that do not need higher throughput (such a terminal emulation data collection applications), an installed 900 MHz wireless LAN continues to provide return on investment.

2.4 GHz

2.4 GHz is more of a worldwide band, because there are no existing allocations of the band in Japan or Europe (except for part of the band in France). While there are nuances associated with a global implementation, what used to require vendors to have two different radios can now be integrated into a single global radio.

Non-standards based 2.4 GHz

Similar to the 900 MHz band, there was no standard for initial implementations in 2.4 GHz. Products such as Symbol's Spectrum24, Proxim's RangeLAN2 and solutions from Aironet (Cisco) provided the foundation that many companies used to build their wireless infrastructure. Other companies that provided vertical market solutions (such as Teklogix, LXE and Intermec) used multiple radios built by themselves or other companies. Additionally, some versions of access points allowed the internal radio (usually a PC card) to be changed in the factory, providing a migration path as radio technology changed. This architecture allows them to add the differentiation for their wireless solutions on top of the physical radio.

Proxim and WLIF

In the mid-1990's, a consortium of companies formed the Wireless LAN Interoperability Forum (WLIF). These companies based their products on Proxim's RangeLAN2 suite of products. WLIF was the first organization that allowed customers to pick access points and mobile clients from more than one vendor, though it was based on a single vendor's radio and protocol. With hundreds of interoperable products on the market, WLIF challenged the IEEE 802.11 working group, who at the time continued to work on an overdue standard. With the introduction of the IEEE 802.11 standard, WLIF and its associated products have been replaced. Today, WLIF no longer exists.

HomeRF

The HomeRF Working Group Inc. (HRFWG) was formed to establish the mass deployment of interoperable wireless networking access devices to both local content and the Internet for voice, data and streaming media in consumer environments. It is very similar to WLIF because it is built on the foundation of Proxim's RangeLAN2 specification. The HRFWG includes the

leading companies from the personal computer, consumer electronics, peripherals, communications, software, and semiconductor industries.

HomeRF operates in the 2.4GHz band and uses frequency-hopping technology. Effective August 2000, the FCC approved the use of wide band frequency hopping. The lack of being able to use a wider band limited the
capability of FH to reach the 11 Mbps speed of DS, which is one of the reasons
why FH was not included in the IEEE 802.11b specification for high-speed
wireless. The new FCC rules allow the HomeRF FH implementation to reach
10 Mbps throughput, which falls back to 5 Mbps and then to the original
RangeLAN2 throughput of 1.6 Mbps and .8 Mbps. While the new FCC rules
allow FH technology to break the 10 Mbps barrier using a wider frequency
spectrum than its IEEE 802.11 DS counterpart, FCC limitations on power output mean that there is no coverage advantage to implementing a HomeRF
solution. Today, HomeRF is no longer a factor as an implementation choice for
wireless solutions.

Bluetooth

The Bluetooth™ wireless technology has been set to revolutionize the personal connectivity market by providing freedom from wired connections. It is
a specification for a small-form factor, low-cost radio solution, providing links
between mobile computers, mobile phones and other portable handheld
devices. The Bluetooth Special Interest Group (SIG), comprised of leaders in
the telecommunications, computing, and network industries, is driving development of the technology and bringing it to market. The Bluetooth SIG
includes promoter companies 3Com, Ericsson, IBM, Intel, Lucent, Microsoft,
Motorola, Nokia and Toshiba, and more than 2000 Adopter/Associate member
companies.[1]

The first versions of Bluetooth specification were released in early 1999 and
consisted of three radio definitions using frequency hopping with a scheme of
1600 hops per second. The most popular is lower power radio (only one hun-
dredth of the output of 802.11b) that provides a personal wireless connection
within 10 meters. Whereas 802.11b supports only Ethernet-like applications,
Bluetooth is likely to be supported in a far wider range of peripherals, including mobile phones, PDAs and printers, with the intent to replace the cable that
typically connects these devices.

---

1 From Bluetooth homepage, www.bluetooth.org

STANDARDS BASED

The Institute of Electrical and Electronic Engineers (IEEE) is an international organization that has a charter to create standards. These standards are created by groups of people who volunteer their time and represent many different organizations, including academics, business, military and the government. The standard for wireless communication is part of a family of standards for LAN/MAN Standards Committee (LMSC). The LMSC or IEEE project 802 deals with the physical and data link layers of communication as defined by the ISO (International Standards Organization) OSI (Open Systems Interconnection) basic reference model. There are many different working groups with IEEE 802, and while not all of the groups are currently working on standards activities, the following groups have charters with IEEE 802:

	Working Groups
802.1	High Level Interface (Bridging)
802.2	Logical Link Control
802.3	CDMA/CD (Ethernet)
802.4	Token Bus
802.5	Token Ring
802.6	Metropolitan Area Network
802.7	Broadband
802.8	Fiber Optic (FOTAG)
802.9	Integrated Services (ISLAN)
802.10	Interoperable LAN Security (SILS)
802.11	Wireless LAN
802.12	Demand Priority
802.13	None
802.14	Cable TV Based Broadband
802.15	Wireless Personal Area Network
802.16	Broadband Wireless Access
802.17	Resilient Packet Ring
802.18	Radio Regulatory
802.19	Coexistence Technical Group

IEEE 802.11

In July 1996, the IEEE 802.11 Wireless LAN standard passed in the working committee with virtually unanimous consent. Product adhering to the standard is interoperable at a radio level. In order to reach true interoperability, manufacturers must undergo interoperability and compliance testing.

As mandated by the LMSC charter, the IEEE 802.11 Wireless LAN standard covers the first two layers of the model's seven layers—the Physical layer (PHY) and Medium Access Control (MAC) layer. The PHY layer describes the properties of the communication medium that can be determined by electrical currents, such as voltages, currents, impedances, rise times, etc. The MAC layer describes data link properties, such as message elements, bus access, data synchronization, error detection, etc. The PHY layers included in the 802.11 standard offer three options: 2.4 GHz direct sequence, frequency hopping spread spectrum radio and infrared technologies.

"Over the air" interoperability will be enabled for each of these three technologies, but interoperability between the technologies is not possible. Direct Sequence (DSSS) devices will communicate only with other DSSS products, and Frequency Hoppers will interoperate only with other FHSS products. The MAC layer for the two technologies is common, but numerous implementation options at the MAC level are allowed, which will make interoperability, even between like PHY layers, a challenge. Because of the myriad possible implementation options, even though products may interoperate, there is a wide variation in the performance of products. This performance ranges in coverage, power draw and size of the radio.

The 802.11 standard covers **only** the activity over-the-air, not what happens between the APs that are attached, or connected, to the Distribution System (often an Ethernet network). When a client device registers with an AP for the first time on power-up or when it comes in range, this function is called *Association*. After Association, when the station moves out of range of the initial AP and re-registers with a new AP, this is called *Re-Association*. All that the 802.11 standard says about Re-Association, as it relates to the wired backbone, is that "The AP shall inform the Distribution System of the Re-Association." *This means that the 802.11 standard alone, without something else, does not provide for roaming.* The reason for this is that the functionality of the APs, and how they interact over the Distribution System, is outside the scope or above the jurisdiction of the 802 standards body that has responsibility for the Layers 1 and 2, the PHY and MAC.

802.11 Task Groups

Within 802.11, different task groups continue to build on the standard. As new issues arise, task groups are formed to address them. The following task groups currently exist:

802.11a	The scope of the project is to develop a PHY to operate in the 5 GHz UNII band. Work has been completed on the ISO / IEC version of the original Standard as an amendment—Published as 8802-11: 1999 (E)/Amd 1: 2000 (ISO/IEC) (IEEE Std. 802.11a-1999 Edition)
802.11b	The scope of the project is to develop a standard for a higher rate PHY in the 2.4GHz band. Work has been completed and is now part of the Standard as an amendment—Published as IEEE Std. 802.11b-1999.
802.11b-cor1	The scope of this project is to correct deficiencies in the MIB definition of 802.11b. Work has been completed and is now part of the Standard as an amendment—Published as IEEE Std. 802.11b-cor1 2001
802.11c	To add a subclause under 2.5 Support of the Internal Sub-Layer Service by specific MAC Procedures to cover bridge operation with IEEE 802.11 MAC. This supplement to ISO/IEC 10038 (IEEE 802.1D) will be developed by the 802.11 Working Group in cooperation with the IEEE 802.1 Working Group. Work has been completed and is now part of the ISO/IEC 10038 (IEEE 802.1D) Standard
802.11d	This supplement will define the physical layer requirements (channelization, hopping patterns, new values for current MIB attributes, and other requirements to extend the operation of 802.11 WLANs to new regulatory domains (countries). Work has been completed and is now part of the Standard as an amendment—Published as IEEE Std. 802.11d 2001
802.11e	Enhance the 802.11 Medium Access Control (MAC) to improve and manage Quality of Service, provide classes of service, and enhanced security and authentication mechanisms. Consider efficiency enhancements in the areas of the Distributed Coordination Function (DCF) and Point Coordination Function (PCF).

802.11f	To develop recommended practices for an Inter-Access Point Protocol (IAPP)
802.11g	To develop a higher speed physical layer extension to 802.11b using the 802.11 MAC
802.11h	To enhance the current 802.11 MAC and 802.11a PHY with network management and control extensions for spectrum and transmit power management in 5GHz license exempt bands, enabling regulatory acceptance of 802.11 5GHz products.
802.11i	Enhance the 802.11 Medium Access Control (MAC) to enhance security and authentication mechanisms

IEEE 802.11b

Even during the IEEE working group celebrations in Hawaii regarding the IEEE 802.11 standard, many engineers were working on the next big step. Modulation schemes allowed the technology to expand beyond the 2 Mbps boundary of the standard. Additionally, the anticipation of a wireless standard had spurred new applications for wireless. But while wireless was growing, some IT administrators were concerned about the performance of applications and potential bottlenecks associated with going from a 10 Mbps Ethernet link to a 2 Mbps wireless link to the mobile clients. IEEE 802.11b had a much easier time going through the working group than the original standard. Part of the decreased time can be attributed to simplification, because 802.11b allowed for only one physical layer implementation. In the original standard, there were three physical layer implementations: direct sequence, frequency hopping and infrared. In the 802.11b standard, only direct sequence is described. One benefit of 802.11b compliant devices is that they are backward-compatible to direct sequence 802.11 devices. This means that while 802.11b devices can communicate with 802.11b devices at 11 Mbps or 5.5 Mbps, they can communicate with 802.11b as well as 802.11 devices at 2 Mbps or 1 Mbps data rates.

IEEE 802.11a

The IEEE 802.11a standard describes wireless LAN operation in the 5 GHz ISM band. This also coordinates with the UNII bands. These radios achieve a 6, 9, 12, 18, 24, 36, 48 or 54 Mbps data rate. Techniques such as rate doubling have allowed proprietary implementations up to 108 Mbps. The 802.11a implementation is not compatible with either 802.11 or 802.11b radios, chiefly because the communication is in a different spectrum (5 GHz versus 2.4 GHz).

IEEE 802.11g

802.11g provides the same data rates as 802.11a, coupled with backwards compatibility to the 802.11b devices. This means that 802.11g devices will operate in the 2.4GHz ISM band. While 802.11g devices will use QPSK (Quadrature Phase Shift Keying) to communicate to 802.11 (1 and 2 Mbps) and 802.11b (1, 2, 5.5 and 11 Mbps), it will switch to Orthogonal Frequency Division Multiplexing (OFDM) modulation technology to achieve 54 Mbps data rates. As technology matures, chip sets will integrate 802.11b and g at a minimum with the expectation that a, b and g will be capable within a single chip set.

	802.11	802.11a	802.11b	802.11g
Standard Approved	July 1996	September 1999	September 1999	2003
Available Bandwidth	83.5 MHz	300 MHz	83.5 MHz	83.5 MHz
Unlicensed Frequencies of Operation	2.4-2.4835 GHz	5.15-5.35 GHz 5.725-5.825 GHz	2.4-2.4835 GHz	2.4-2.4835 GHz
Number of Non-Overlapping Channels	3 (Indoor/Outdoor)	4 Indoor (UNII1) 4 Indoor/Outd oor (UNII2) 4 Outdoor (UNII3)	3 (Indoor/Out door)	3 (Indoor/Out door)
Data Rate per Channel	2, 1 Mbps	54, 48, 36, 24, 12, 9, 6 Mbps	11, 5.5, 2, 1 Mbps	54, 36, 33, 24, 22, 12, 11, 5.5 2, 1 Mbps
Compatibility	802.11		802.11 and 802.11b	802.11g, 802.11 and 802.11b

MAJOR WIRELESS ORIENTED ORGANIZATIONS: WI-FI

As the wireless industry continues to expand, several industry organizations have been developed to provide and contribute to the growth and education in the wireless LAN marketplace. Originally known as the Wireless Ethernet Compatibility Alliance (WECA), Wi-Fi is a trade name for an industry trade group called the Wi-Fi Alliance. The charter promotes and tests for wireless

LAN interoperability of 802.11b and 802.11a devices. Wi-Fi's mission is to certify interoperability of Wi-Fi (IEEE 802.11) products and to promote Wi-Fi as the global wireless LAN standard across all market segments.

When a product meets the interoperability requirements as described in Wi-Fi's test matrix, WECA grants the product certification of interoperability, which allows the vendor to use the Wi-Fi logo on advertising and packaging for the certified product. The Wi-Fi seal of approval assures the end user of interoperability with other wireless LAN devices that also bear the Wi-Fi logo. The website is www.wirelessethernet.org.

Questions and Useful Tips

❖ *Where can I find information about standards-based wireless solutions?*
  ➢ The Wi-Fi Alliance provides general information about the wireless market and also provides certification testing and assures that all products with the Wi-Fi logo can communicate. In addition to these industry organizations, there are many colleges and universities that have set up groups to do research on a variety of issues in the wireless LAN space.

❖ *Should I upgrade my currently installed UHF or 900 MHz wireless network?*
  ➢ There are two steps in answering this question. The first step deals with regulations, with the changing in the UHF band that requires compliance to Part 88—some older UHF systems will need to be upgraded. Secondly, this is a business question. Because this solution is a proprietary solution, it relies on a single vendor. The biggest question is the ability to get service and maintain the solution, assuming that the communication needs have not outstripped the capacity of the current network. With the decreasing costs of standards based wireless technology, it is recommended that any new requirements be deployed with a standards-based solution. What is good about the current standards-based solutions is that they can overlay any current solution that has been deployed. Once the older system is not cost effective, the additional requirements can be upgraded to the standards-based solution.

❖ *Should I look at UHF or 900 MHz for a new application?*
  ➢ It is important to understand the applications that are using wireless within the business before moving ahead to deploy additional wireless solutions. Standards-based wireless, such as IEEE 802.11b, should be the foundation for any in-premise wireless architecture. Proprietary

wireless solutions tie the company to a single vendor and are costly. The only exception is for special purpose operations, such as covering a large outdoor port that is not moving very much information. In this case, a proprietary UHF solution meets the business needs and is much more cost effective than setting up eight to ten times more access points for coverage.

❖ *Do HomeRF, Bluetooth and IEEE 802.11 radios interoperate?*

➤ No. While the radio frequency is the same, the communication protocols differ.

❖ *Can I roam from one IEEE 802.11 or .11b access point to another?*

➤ It depends. If both access points are from the same vendor, then the answer is yes, because the vendor has established an inter-access point protocol that allows both access points to communicate. Because there is no documented standard for inter-access point protocol (IAPP), access points from different vendors cannot pass a roaming client from one vendor's access point to another. This means that while at the radio layer the radios can move from one access point to another the network connection and session established by the application cannot be transferred. It will require (at a minimum) retries, and possibly relogging into the network resource.

❖ *Should I use Bluetooth for my access point infrastructure?*

➤ The Bluetooth specification allows for several different types of radios, namely a personal area LAN that uses 10 mW and a definition for a 100 mW solution for infrastructures. Most wireless LAN vendors continue to use IEEE 802.11 technology instead of Bluetooth for access point infrastructure communications. So, technically yes, though an IEEE 802.11b/g may be a better business solution.

❖ *Can I still purchase a UHF solution? Does it still require a license from the FCC?*

➤ Yes. For wide-open areas such as ship yards, ports or rail yards where it can support applications that require a large coverage area and also have low data throughput, you must obtain a license. Synthesized UHF radios are integrated into access points and have many of the same functions as standards based 2.4 GHz solutions. The significantly reduced number of access points needed to cover the area usually offsets the higher costs of the radio and the wireless solution.

❖ *Do I need a license to operate a spread spectrum radio?*

➤ In most cases, a license is not required to operate a spread spectrum device. In the US, spread spectrum devices fall under FCC Part 15 of the rules that govern unlicensed devices. However, other countries may require a license if you are operating devices that are partially or completely outdoors, such as point-to-point bridges. In addition, some countries may require the system importer to obtain a telecommunications license to sell the product.

❖ *Would a frequency hopping (FH) radio sitting next to a direct sequence (DS) radio have any negative effect?*

➤ Yes. By its very nature, an FH product hops across the entire band. It will therefore spend time encountering interference from the DS solution and causing interference to the FH solution. There is no way to control where an FH unit will hop. Blocking out the portion of the spectrum that the equipment uses would be a possible solution, but in the United States the FCC does not permit FH devices to limit their hop—they must hop across the whole band.

❖ *How do I know if my equipment is FCC certified?*

➤ If your equipment is FCC certified, there will be an FCC certification number. Manufacturers must certify that the equipment complies with FCC Part 15 rules, and it is subject to the following two conditions:

▪ The device may not cause harmful interference.

▪ The device must accept any interference received, including interference that may cause undesired operation.

❖ *If I want to change mobile clients that are using terminal emulation, are there any issues of which I need to be aware?*

➤ Yes, it is important to be careful. Some host applications, particularly warehouse management and enterprise resource planning (ERP) software packages, had special drivers written that utilized proprietary commands that are not part of the terminal emulation data stream, or work with certain screen sizes even if it is a direct connect implementation and there is no gateway involved. It is wise to check any changes with the application vendor and to test the application thoroughly before deploying.

❖ *Do I need to keep track of all of the IEEE 802.11 Task Groups?*

➤ No, not specifically. When you are looking at deploying a technology it is important to understand the functionality that is needed for your application. Reviewing the working groups in 802.11 can give you information about where the market is going and the products that are coming to the market in the future.

❖ *Can I use any IEEE 802.11 product for my wireless solution?*

➤ Technically yes, but the system will function at the least common denominator of functionality in respect to the standard as it is defined. Trade-off between performance and interoperability do exist. As a result if performance is an important metric to the success of the project, single vendor network tend to provide the best overall performance in respect to data rate, throughput and range.

❖ *If a device is Wi-Fi certified, will it provide all of the functionality noted on another Wi-Fi certified access point?*

➢ Interoperability between Wi-Fi devices is a matter of degrees. Because the standard has many different options, it cannot be guaranteed that the device and the access point will support all of the same options. The Wi-Fi Alliance serves to provide a level of performance assurance based on the baseline testing that is done on each Wi-Fi component.

Radio Fundamentals

From the beginning

Radio frequencies (RF) are high frequency alternating current (AC) signals that are passed along a cable and then radiated into the air via an antenna. An antenna converts a wired signal into a wireless signal as it transmits (and vice versa when a signal is received from another source). When the signal is transmitted from the antenna, it forms radio waves. The waves are formed much the same way they would be if a stone were dropped into a lake.

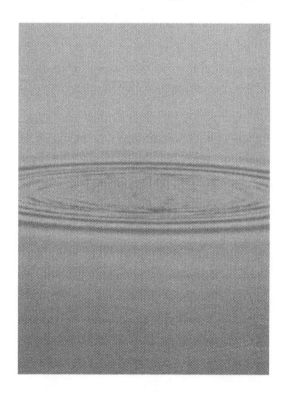

What is radio frequency (RF) communication?

The radio component of a wireless solution moves information from one place to another through the air. There are many different types of radios operating in many different frequencies and varying form factors. While there are many variables of radio design that are used to differentiate them in the marketplace, the basic physics behind the operation is the same; we can derive baselines that can be used to compare all radios. The two biggest features (and the most common for comparisons) between differing radio communications portion of wireless solutions are coverage and performance. Understanding how to calculate the estimated radio coverage of any area for wireless communication consideration allows the IT team to understand the number of access points that may be needed, whether there is a red flag based on the site survey results and the total costs for the return on investment analysis. Within the radio communications element of the solution, there are three basic components: the transmitter, the receiver and the radio waves that traverse the environment between the transmitter and the receiver.

Transmitter

The most important aspect of a transmitter is the power or energy that is used to send the information. The power output of a transmitter with the cables to the antenna (but without the antenna) is defined by the FCC as an intentional radiator (IR), while the power output *with* the antenna is equivalent isotropically radiated power (EIRP). There are regulations concerning intentional radiators and EIRP to which wireless vendors must conform, but they differ from frequency band to frequency band. While vendors conform to intentional radiator regulations, **implementers and end users** need to be aware of equivalent isotropically radiated power (EIRP) that is installed when cables, splitters, amplifiers and antennas are added to the installed system.

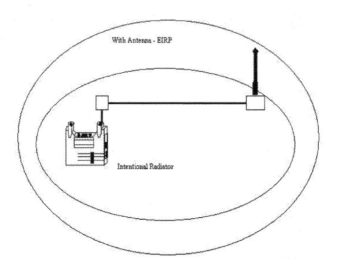

While maximum power output can mean better coverage, it also means more power usage (or battery power for mobile handhelds).

CALCULATING EIRP

The first step to determining the total power output, or EIRP, is to get to a common unit of measure because the output from the intentional radiator (radio) is measured in watts or milliwatts ($1/1000^{th}$ watt) and cable loss is measured in decibels (dB). Milliwatts are the unit of measure given for the intentional radiator.

Units of Measure

The first step is to clarify the definitions before beginning the process of converting from one to another:

Watt	A standard unit of measure that is used to express the rate that power is dissipated. A milliwatt (mW) is $1/1000^{th}$ of a watt.
Decibel (dB)	A logarithmic express of the ratio between two signals' output power
dBm	Decibels referenced to 1 mW for example a 1 mW signal has a level of 0 dBm
dBi	Decibels referenced from the to the gain of antenna

Watt A standard unit of measure that is used to express the rate that power is dissipated. A milliwatt (mW) is $1/1000^{th}$ of a watt. Decibel (dB) A logarithmic express of the ratio between two signals' output power dBm Decibels referenced to 1 mW for example a 1 mW signal has a level of 0 dBm dBi Decibels referenced from the to the gain of antenna

The gain and loss are measured in decibels, not in watts, because gain and loss are relative concepts that are applied to absolute power measurement. The decibels are noted as dBm because the reference is in milliwatts (as opposed to dB where the reference is watts).

Radio Frequency Math Relationships

With the definitions in hand, the following mathematical relationship allows the conversion of power measurements from dBm to mW and vise versa. When we start with output power measured in milliwatts (mW), the equation is as follows:

$$\text{Power}_{dbm} = 10\log_{\text{Power(mw)}}$$

Conversely, when we start with dBm, the equation is as follows:

$$P_{mW} = \log^{-1}\left(\frac{P_{dBm}}{10}\right)$$

The following logarithmic table provides approximations for most of the values needed for common conversions:

mW	dBm
1	0
2	3
4	6
8	9
10	10
16	12
32	15
64	18
100 mW	20
128	21
256	24
512 or ~500 mW	27
1024 or ~ 1W	30
2W	33
4w	36

Because this is a logarithmic relationship, the delta is 1.28 mW per 1 dB can be used to extrapolate other logarithmic values that may be needed.

Adding the Antenna Gain to the Equation

While gain and loss of the cable and connectors from the intentional radiator are expressed in dBm, the antenna gain is expressed in dBi, where the "i" stands for isotropic. As with dBm, dBi measurements are relative to the power source, which is always positive because antennas cannot degrade the signal.

A sample circuit may include a 100 mW intentional radiator source at 2.4 GHz in the ISM band with two connectors that connect a cable from the radio to the antenna. Additional information needed is that cable is low loss (so the loss is negligible) and the connectors have -3 dB loss associated. Lastly, a 9 dBi gain antenna is connected to the cable.

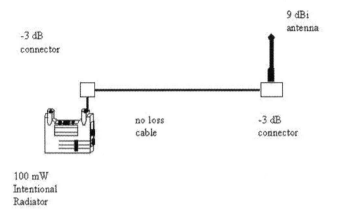

9 dBi
antenna

-3 dB
connector

no loss
cable

-3 dB
connector

100 mW
Intentional
Radiator

First to calculate the EIRP in dBm, the equation is as follows:

EIRP = IR + connector loss + cable loss + connector loss + antenna gain

EIRP = 100 mW + (-3 dBm) + 0 +(-3 dBm) + 9dBi

100 mW = 20 dBm (from the log table)

20 dBm+ - 3 dB + - 3 dB + 9 dB = 23 dBm

Converting back from the log table, 23 dBm is approximately 200 mW.

Calculating the same EIRP circuit in mW, the base equation stays the same but the calculation is a little different:

EIRP = IR + connector loss + cable loss + connector loss + antenna gain

EIRP = 100 mW + (-3 dB) + 0 +(-3 dB) + 9dBi

EIRP = 100 mW + 3 dB

A 3 dB gain has the effect of doubling the available output power. In this case, 100 mW would be doubled to 200 mW. In this example, the EIRP is 200 mW, which is well below the 4 watt maximum for 2.4 GHZ radios operating in the ISM band.

dBm to mW Reference Numbers

As a quick and easy reference, IT administrators should be familiar with the following dBm to mW reference numbers:
- - 3 dB = half of the power in mW
- +3 dB = double the power in mW
- -10 dB = one tenth of the power in mW
- +10 dB = ten times the power in mW

Another Math Example

The IR is 100 mW, the cable and associated connectors equals—3dB and the antenna has a 10 dBi gain.

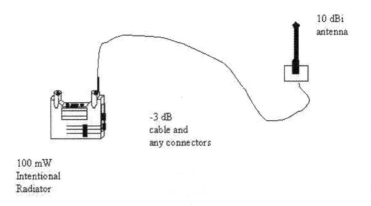

EIRP = IR + connector loss + cable loss + connector loss + antenna gain

EIRP = 100 mW + (-3 dB) + 10 dBi

Using the dB to mW reference numbers, 100 mW is converted to 50 mW because - 3 dB reduces the available energy by ½ but as the energy reaches the antenna it is amplified by 10X and the resulting power is 500 mW. We could have reached the same conclusion by taking the 100 mW + 7 dB and seeing that 7 dB is approximately a 5.28 multiplier of 100 mW or ~528 mW.

Turning it around to convert mW to dB:

EIRP = IR + connector loss + cable loss + connector loss + antenna gain

EIRP = 100 mW + (-3 dB) + 10 dBi

= 20 dBm + 7 dB

= 27 dBm

and back to the log chart 27 dBm equals ~ 500 mW.

Receiver

The receiver has the responsibility of gathering the signal from the coverage area and converting it to a digital format that can be interpreted. There are several issues that effect how the radio signal is received, such as the data rate, the modulation of the signal and the quality of radio implementation. These issues are used to calculate a quality called *receiver sensitivity*. Receiver sensitivity is measured by dBm, and is typically a negative number. Continuing with the IEEE 802.11 radio analogy, the receiver sensitivity for 2.4 GHz 802.11 radio will be approximately -85 dBm. This information can be requested from the vendor, and if coverage is an important piece of the technical decision making process, it is recommended that this analysis be completed.

Link Margin

Link margin is a simple equation of subtracting the receiver sensitivity of the receiver from the amount of energy used to send the information by the transmitter (EIRP). Link margin is the amount of energy that is used to push and/or pull the data through the wireless medium. Calculating the link margin of our example 802.11 radio:

$$20 \text{ dBm} - (-85 \text{ dBm}) = 105 \text{ dBm of energy}$$

How to Improve Link Margin

The better the link margin, the better the coverage of the radio. The output energy that represents the communications signal can be affected or tweaked. For many years, manufacturers have tweaked the signal to get the desired marketing results. One can increase the transmit power (as Proxim and Symbol did with 500 mW 2.4 GHz proprietary access points). One can also decrease the data rate, which is part of the IEEE 802.11 standard and allows the throughput to change from 11 Mbps down to 1 Mbps, with the understanding that the coverage of 11 Mbps is significantly less than 1 Mbps.

Increase the Transmit Power

In order to improve coverage, some companies offer a 500mW radio instead of a 100 mW radio. This increases the transmit power contribution to the link margin equation. The basic premise is that more energy equals more coverage. It is important to note that if the transmit power is increased that every radio in the wireless system support the new transmit power setting and be changed to it, or the corresponding receiver sensitivity needs to be adjusted. Imagine an access point that increases its transmit power to 500 mW while the client remains at 100 mW. While the client will be able to hear the access point, it may not be able to talk to it because its signal is too weak to reach it. If the access point supports automatic transmit power adjustment capabilities to assure that there are no coverage holes, it is important to make sure that there is a communication message that is supported between the client and the access point to assure there is not a transmit power mismatch.

Decrease the Data Rate

In order to get better coverage, companies may reduce data rate, in 900 MHz solutions varied from 350 Kbps to 60 Kbps, which creates longer slots to transmit and receive data. This means that there will be fewer retries for the data.

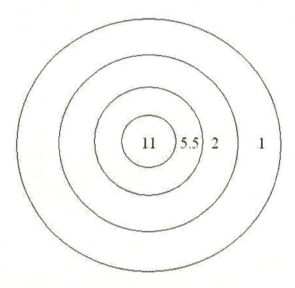

In 2.4 GHz solutions, increased coverage can be seen when an IEEE 802.11 radio data rate decreases as the data rate decreases from 11 Mbps to 5.5 Mbps to 2 Mbps to 1 Mbps. In most radios, this degradation of data rate is automatic. It is important to be able to lock in the appropriate data rate if the higher rate is needed. It is also important to be able to lock in the data rate because if a site survey for an 11 Mbps solution is completed, it will contain many more access points / radios than a 2 or 1 Mbps site survey. If the radios in the 11 Mbps survey are allowed to auto-fallback to the slower data rate, clients will potentially see three to five (or more) access point signals, and may spend more time switching access points for the wired connection than transferring data.

Increase Frequency Diversity

This applies only to frequency hopping solutions and means increasing the number of hops that the radio makes per second. While the IEEE 802.11 standard specifies the number of hops to allow interoperability, proprietary implementations at 900 MHz were not bound by this rule and were allowed to modify the frequency diversity.

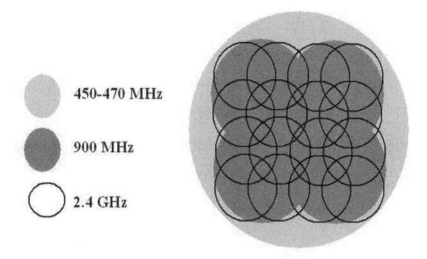

450-470 MHz

900 MHz

2.4 GHz

Decrease Antenna Diversity

Some manufacturers will use antenna diversity to improve the performance against interference that may occur in the environment at the sacrifice of coverage. If the installation is in an environment that does not have interference (based on information from the site survey or individual testing) and the access point has antenna diversity (two antennas on the access point), check the access point documentation because many manufacturers allow this to be disabled in the set up of the access point.

Decrease the Frequency

While decreasing the frequency does not add or increase link margin, at lower frequencies a lesser amount of link margin is used to double the coverage area. This means that the same link margin (for example 105 dBm of energy) will go further at 900 MHz than at 2.4 GHz. The implementation of decreasing the frequency may require totally different equipment for the wireless installation and should be made only during the design stages of the wireless network.

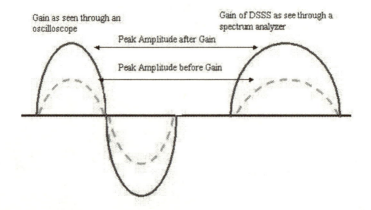

Add Gain Antennas

Gain antennas are like signal amplifiers, which create additional link margin and therefore allow the stronger signal to go farther. Gain, when used in conjunction with radio frequency, is used to describe an *increase* in the amplitude of the signal. While gain antennas are commonly used in North America, it is important to note that gain antennas are not allowed for use in European countries. In Europe, all access points are shipped with 0 dB gain antennas. This will increase the number of access points that are needed to cover similar facilities comparatively from the US to Europe. This increase can occur intentionally when an RF amplifier is used to amplify the signal or when a *gain* antenna is used. This is done to increase the coverage.

Sometimes gain occurs where it may not be wanted, such as when two reflected signals come together. If the radio waves are not in phase, this can cause multi-pathing or a null where the two signals will cancel each other. If the signals are in phase, the amplitude will increase and provide increased coverage. While in most cases this may be good, legally it can pose problems if the power of the new wave exceeds regulatory limitations.

There are two issues that limit the universal implementation of gain antennas. The first is that the more gain, the more expensive the antenna. Secondly, the more gain the larger the antenna. In the days when UHF or 900 MHz systems were prevalent, gain antennas were put on access points because it was cheaper to add a 5—15 dB antenna that could potentially double the coverage area than to add another access point. While the axiom that gain antennas are the best way to increase coverage works well for UHF and 900 MHz wireless infrastructures, it does not work for 2.4 GHz where the cost of adding another access point is more cost effective.

SIGNAL LOSS

Signal loss is the opposite of gain and describes a decrease in the signal strength. Many things can cause loss, including the cable the signal is traveling on, the connectors and objects that may absorb the signal as it moves through as a wave. Signal loss typically manifests itself as heat and is the opposite effect of trying to improve the link margin, and must be taken into account. Whether it occurs in a cable or an impedance mismatch in two connectors, the amount of signal loss is subtracted from the link margin before the coverage is calculated.

Sometimes there is a need to reduce the amount of link margin. For UHF systems, the coverage area can be very large because of the frequency and the allowed power at which the signal could be transmitted. In many of these wireless installations, attenuators are part of the solution because they are used to reduce the signal (and therefore, the coverage area) to the appropriate size. An attenuator usually attaches to the cable with the antenna and is a circuit that converts that signal to heat in order to reduce the link margin. For example, a single UHF radio may be able to provide coverage for 750,000 to 1 million square feet. If the area that needs coverage is only 300,000 square feet, attenuators would reduce the coverage so that the signal does not expand beyond the coverage area. Another common use of attenuators is at trade shows, where there are many radios in a small area. Again, the attenuator limits that coverage area.

NEAR FIELD PATH LOSS

Whereas link margin describes how much energy the radio has available to send information, near field path loss is what happens to the signal as it moves through the environment and how it dissipates as it travels through the environment. While the link margin calculates the total energy that is being sent out, it is not all being sent in one direction because the radio signal moves away from the antenna in a circle. It is a lot like dropping a rock in lake and creating a wave.

Near field path loss tells the receiver how much of the original energy is received when the wave passes through a point ten feet away from where the rock was dropped, or from where the radio signal was generated (in our case, the antenna).

Frequency	Percentage of Signal Received	dB
450-470 Mhz	1/4000th	36 dB
902-928 Mhz	1/16,000th	42 dB
2.4 GHz	1/100,000th	50 dB
5.7 GHz	1/400,000th	56 dB

Using an IEEE 802.11 radio as an example, when the 2.4 GHz signal is transmitted from the antenna, only 1/100,000[th] of the signal is received by the receiver after the signal has traveled only ten feet. The physics of this loss is simple when you consider that a radio signal is a wave. This means that while the entire signal is used to create the coverage area for the radio, less than .001% of an unmodified signal is actually used for communication.

WORKING PATH LOSS

Still using the 2.4 GHz radio example and the 105 dBm of energy of link margin that we originally had, we need to subtract 50 dBm due to the near field path loss. This is essentially all of the 20 dB of transmit power and about 25% of the receiver sensitivity. This creates what is often called the "working path loss." This is the total amount of energy of the signal that we can process and return to data. The equation for path loss is

$$Path\ loss = 20 * \log 10 \left[\frac{4 * \pi * d}{\lambda} \right] \{dB\}$$

where d is the distance between the two points and λ is the wavelength in the unit of measure as d. In spread spectrum, information in the transmitted signal is seldom concentrated at a single frequency, so the path loss will actually be different for every frequency component in the signal. Fortunately, the ratio of the bandwidth to center frequency is usually small enough not to matter.

Unfortunately, this 55 dBm also assumes that the communication is a "free space" environment or a vacuum, where nothing—including air molecules—can affect the signal as it moves from the antenna to the receiver. We do not live in a vacuum, and therefore we need to take this into account to ascertain the proper radius for the coverage circle calculation.

Over time, different environments and materials have been tested and categorized into path loss exponents. The next step is to apply an axiom, which allows the user to identify the environment he or she is in and, based on the energy available that we calculated from the radio, estimate the coverage of a single access point. There is no magic to this simple table.

	Frequency		
	450-470 Mhz	902-928 Mhz	2.4 GHz (IEEE 802.11)
Link Margin (TX-RX)[1]	132 to 138 dBm	114 to 120 dBm	105 dBm
Near Field Path Loss	36 dBm	42 dBm	50 dBm
Working Path Lost (Link Margin—Near Field Path Loss)	96 to 102 dBm	72 to 78 dBm	55 dBm
Path Loss Exponents			
$1/R^2$	600-700,000 ft.	40-80,000 ft.	5000 ft.
$1/R^3$	20-40,000 ft.	2500-3500 ft.	600 ft.
$1/R^4$	5000 ft.	650-750 ft.	200-250 ft.
$1/R^5$	800-1100 ft.	300-400 ft.	100-120 ft.
$1/R^6$	400-600 ft.	160-200 ft.	80 ft.

PATH LOSS EXPONENTS

The path loss exponents describe the loss of the signal as it propagates through differing physical environments. Because not every environment is free space or a vacuum, understanding path loss exponents clarifies single radio coverage scenarios and the drop off of coverage as obstacles and changing environments are introduced. This understanding also clarifies why the same signal travels different distances depending on the environment. For example, at 2.4 GHz, moving from an R^4 to an R^5 environment reduces the range from approximately 100,000 square feet to 30,000 square feet because additional obstacles or materials that absorb, refract or reflect radio waves are

---

1. Actual link margin varies from manufacturer to manufacturer.

introduced. This is why site surveys are extremely important, especially at the higher frequencies where there is a lot of volatility associated with coverage.

Obstructions

It would be easy to deploy a wireless solution in a free space environment that does not have to deal with obstacles. This would allow the radio waves from the wireless clients and access points to maintain an omni-directional radiation pattern, making it simpler to predict the maximum operating range for the coverage of an access point. Real world environments are different, and a single facility with multiple access points will have several different obstacles to overcome.

The following table looks at a variety of common materials that compose barriers and how they can affect radio waves. It is easy to see how the same building can move from an R^2 (minimal) or R^3 (low) to an R^5 (high) path loss exponent and why a warehouse with paper products (which has a high path loss exponent) will require more link margin. Therefore, the number of access points that warehouses of the same size (but different products) need can differ greatly.

Component	Path loss exponent	Example
Air	Minimal	
Wood	Low	Pallets, shelves
Synthetic Material	Low	Wall coverings
Asbestos	Low	Ceilings
Glass	Low	Windows
Water, liquids	Medium	
Bricks	Medium	Outer walls
Paper	High	
Concrete	High	Floors and outer walls
Metal	High	Walls, mezzanines, shelves, elevator shafts

Each of the example materials in the table have different characteristics associated with the path loss exponent. Some of the basic issues are reflection, refraction and absorption with respect to the materials. The quantity of the amount of the materials in the coverage area, as well as the type, contributes to the approximation of the path loss component for the environment. It makes sense that a large amount of an obstruction with a low path loss exponent will still cause a noticeable problem with the coverage. For example, a warehouse with a large amount of wood may have greater coverage problems than a warehouse with a small amount of brick.

Reflection

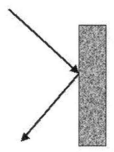

When a wave passes from one medium to another, such as moving through a wall, part or all of the energy of the radio wave is reflected off of the surface. The material that the radio wave is bouncing off of determines the amount of energy that is reflected. Reflection is typically referred to as a wave bouncing off of a surface that is larger than the wavelength of the wave. This means that waves will reflect in one direction.

For example a warehouse with metal walls and a metal roof needs careful planning because placing the antenna too close to the sides or the ceiling can cause multi-pathing, a condition where the reflection causes signal (waves) to cancel each other out or appear larger as they add together.

Scattering

Scattering occurs when the radio waves reflect off of uneven surfaces that are smaller than the wavelength of the radio wave. This means that different portions of the wave will scatter in different directions. Scattering typically occurs when the radio wave bounces off of jagged surfaces or hits random objects such as sand, rocks and trees in an outdoor environment or saw dust or paint in industrial environments.

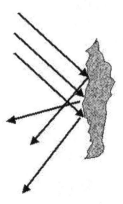

Refraction

Radio waves that go through the walls or bounce off of objects are refracted or have changed their original course. How the radio refracts will depend on the material through which it is going. The scatter of radio waves will create many patterns because most facilities do not consist of uniform materials.

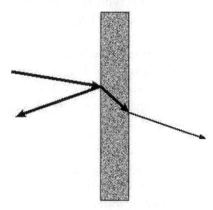

Diffraction

Diffraction is very similar to refraction, and the two terms are often confused. But while refraction describes a wave that bends as it goes through an object, diffraction describes a wave that bends as it goes around an object.

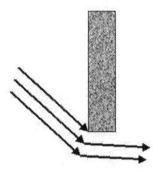

Absorption

Depending on the material that the wave hits, it might be absorbed. Products such as paper or water have a high degree of absorbency. A paper manufacturer or distributor facility can be very difficult to provide uniform wireless communication for because the paper absorbs much of the signal. When the paper is moved, it creates a different coverage pattern that can leave coverage holes. This is the same for businesses that have products that consist of liquids (wine, soda, water, etc.) that may be stacked in warehouses or distribution centers. In office environments, this is a problem only if cubicle walls are installed so that they are close to the ceiling.

The amount of each material also affects the path loss exponent for a specific coverage area, and can be additive from the presence of several different materials in the same location.

Most areas have one or more of the materials in the table in the coverage area, and how much of these materials are present definitely adds to the question.

Spread Spectrum Modulation Techniques

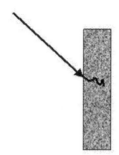

In addition to the amount of energy the signal has that determines the coverage area, the signal uses modulation techniques to communicate the data from one point to another. Products that operate according to Part 15.247 of the FCC's Rules and Regulations must utilize spread spectrum modulation. During World War II, the US military developed spread spectrum techniques to protect communications systems and guided weapons from hostile jamming, though the first use was by ships sent to blockade Cuba in 1962. By operating across a broad range of radio frequencies, a spread spectrum device could manage quite well despite interference from other devices using the same region of the spectrum in the same physical location. Thus, spread spectrum offered a robust method of radio communication that was relatively immune to interference and had a design that made eavesdropping and jamming inherently difficult. The only thing a receiver had to do in order to decode the signal was know the specific spreading pattern of the transmitter.

Two modulation schemes of several developed by the military are approved to be used to encode spread spectrum signals: direct sequence and frequency hopping. The others are chirping, time hopping and hybrids such as time hopping frequency hopping and time hopping direct sequence.

DIRECT SEQUENCE

Direct Sequence Spread Spectrum (DSSS) system implementation can vary. The DSSS system uses a relatively wide channel in both 900 MHz and 2.4 GHz solutions. The full channel can be used to get high throughput, or it can be channelized into smaller pieces, which allows it to be moved if there is any interference.

Interference immunity results from sending each bit redundantly 11 or more times. The FCC requires a minimum of 11. Radio solutions may send each bit more; most commercial implementations send less than 20. Increasing the number of chips per bit from 11 can increase interference immunity, but also increases the cost of the radio implementation.

Processing gain is a direct consequence of the direct sequence radio signal spreading and despreading process. It refers to the increase in signal-to-noise ratio that results from this process, and is required for successful data communications. Processing gain increases as the number of chips per data bit increases, and this can be manipulated by the system designer to get the desired effect. The higher the processing gain, the better the coverage and/or performance of the radio.

FREQUENCY HOPPING

Frequency Hopping Spread Spectrum (FHSS) systems allow for a variety of implementations. A 2.4 GHz Frequency Hopping Spread Spectrum system uses 79 one MHz wide channels and "hops" around the entire band, using a pseudo-random sequence. All units in a given cell must hop around at the same time. Each device hops around in a random sequence, but they must be synchronized. This is accomplished by all of the units knowing the pattern of hopping as well as the duration and the current time of each hop.

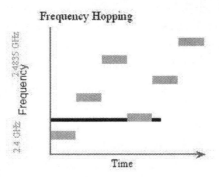

An FHSS system obtains its interference immunity from the fact that by moving around the band rapidly it can avoid interference much of the time. Rather than send data redundantly across the entire data channel, as in DSSS, the FHSS system sends packets of data and checks them for errors. If an error in a packet occurs, the packet is re-transmitted, often in another hop.

The FCC allows FH systems to define their own channel spacing up to a maximum 500 KHz bandwidth in the 900 MHz band, or a 1 MHz bandwidth in the 2.4 GHz band. There are also FCC requirements on the amount of time the transmitter can spend on any one channel, and the number of channels that must be used. This is done to avoid "collisions" between different transmitters.

Rule Changes for FCC

On August 31, 2000, the FCC created a new rule regarding FHSS to allow for wide band frequency hopping. The FCC rule changes consist of the following:

OLD RULES

- minimum 75 hops in a sequence
- 1 W output power in point to multi-point systems
- 1 MHz maximum carrier frequency bandwidth

NEW RULES

- minimum 15 hops in a sequence
- 125 mW output power
- 5 Mhz maximum carrier frequency bandwidth

While these rule changes allowed for higher throughput in FHSS wireless communication, the decreased power, a factor of 8 times, caused range issues that meant it still did not have any advantages competing head to head with DSSS in enterprise solutions.

STRENGTHS AND WEAKNESSES OF DSSS AND FHSS RADIO TECHNOLOGIES

Wireless LAN vendors have debated the merits of the two spread spectrum techniques for a number of years. Typically, the arguments have been slanted to favor the technology that an individual vendor manufactures. There are no overriding advantages to either direct sequence or frequency hopping. Both can be made to work and be competitive in the market. The following are some of the strengths and weaknesses of each technology.

Lower overhead/complexity

A frequency hopping system uses some percentage of the available signaling bandwidth to establish and maintain synchronization. Typically, this is as much as 10-20% of the available bandwidth. A direct sequence system will use 5-10% bandwidth for the same function.

Simple Roaming

You may extend coverage of a direct sequence system by installing additional access points—using the same DS spreading sequence. Roaming in this case is simple; a roaming unit can monitor or attempt to access all access points within range. As it moves out of the coverage area of one access point, it can readily find another by executing a simple search algorithm. Complexity of roaming may increase if a DSSS system is channelized into three or four frequency channels to improve capacity. Frequency hopping systems will not generally use the sample-hopping pattern in adjacent access points because of interference and coordination limitations. Roaming units in an FHSS system must scan other hopping sequences to change access points. This requires a specialized search algorithm, and may require substantial periods of time in some cases. Most FHSS system will minimize this issue through various forms of aided acquisition techniques, such as periodically communicating synchronization information over the RF link.

Wireless Access Points

Using a single frequency, single sequence DSSS operation makes it easy to employ wireless access points. Access points allow mobile computers to attach, but maintain a wireless connection to the wired backbone by communicating to other access points. While in proprietary implementation this is accomplished using a single radio (and therefore, lower the cost), wireless distribution system functionality in IEEE 802.11 uses two radios. In FHSS systems, an access point participates in two coverage areas and therefore two radios (using two hopping sequences) simultaneously provide this function, potentially a complex and low performance solution. This functionality needs to be evaluated on a per-band basis because the coverage needed to accommodate wireless bases is approximately 40%, which would significantly increase the number of access points at 2.4 GHz. Additionally, the hop adds to the throughput because there would be two wireless communications of the message. This increased response time needs to be considered for UHF wireless access points.

Interference

FHSS has more interference immunity than DSSS, especially at 2.4 GHz. A common analogy utilizes a series of trains to explain the concept. In a DSSS implementation that payload (data) is spread out equally among the trains which all depart at the same time. At the receiver, the trains arrive at the same time and the data is unloaded. Duplication of the data is common so that when the data arrives corrupted due to interference a redundant message fills in the gap. In an FHSS implementation, the trains leave at different times on the different tracks. If a train runs into interference that track is simply not used until the interference no longer impedes the train from reaching the destination (receiver). Because interference tends to cover more than one channel a DSSS implementation will lose more of its payload (data) because the trains are sent out over sequential tracks than a FHSS implementation where the tracks are sent out in non-sequential order.

Power Management

DSSS solutions must operate their clocks at five to ten times the bit rate. Power consumption in integrated circuits increases with increasing clock speed, making direct sequence receivers more power hungry than FHSS. Both types of receivers must be power managed. An important trade off to note is that while DSSS solutions will consume more power during the transmit time but FHSS solutions must be kept on longer due to longer synchronization periods. Typically a 2.4 GHz DSSS radio will have better battery life than a comparable 2.4 GHz FHSS counterpart.

Scalability

While both FHSS and DSSS are scalable, frequency hopping is more scalable than direct sequence. This is based on the notion of using multiple data channels in each cell to increase the overall data capacity available to users in a given cell of coverage. At 2.4 GHz, a DSSS system has an absolute limit of three non-overlapping channels, and therefore by stacking three access points in a cell the total capacity is available. Depending on the radio band used, this can be as little as 180 Kbps for three 60 Kbps 900 MHz solutions to a combined 6 Mbps for a (3) three 2 Mbps 2.4 GHz solution or 30 Mbps for (3) three IEEE

802.11b access points set to 11 Mbps. The key is to understand the required bandwidth for the application.

With FHSS, this upper limit is much more difficult to determine. Commercial FHSS implementations today define 78 possible hopping sequences. Some vendors have claimed that 25 Mbps of capacity is possible through the co-location of many access points, but these claims are naive and not based on sound engineering or analysis. The real answer to scalability requires a thorough analysis of the impact of co-locating FHSS access points. The FHSS hopping sequences are designed so that if any two hopping sequences are used, a collision on the same channel will occur only once during the time the two access points would hop through the entire sequence. But in the real world, the collisions are much greater than that and realistically there is throughput fall off after 8 to 9 Mbps throughput no matter the number of FHSS access points.

Radio Design Issues in WLAN

There are several key issues that need to be taken into account when a wireless solution is designed. Setting the expectation associated with each of these issues will lead to a successful wireless implementation. While advances in technology have tried to assist in addressing the basic problems introduced, without a proper understanding of the following design issues you may slow performance.

SPATIAL REUSE

Access points that cover different disjoint areas of the facility have the capability of wirelessly communicating with the mobile clients at the same time in their coverage area. These access points will buffer the communication as they bridge the information onto the Ethernet. This "spatial reuse" capability was very important when there was only a limited amount of radio data bandwidth, but it is used with every frequency band and is a benefit of the CDMA architecture. In the early days, when radio solutions used hub and spoke architectures, controllers polled the mobile clients and spatial reuse was not an option. With the wireless bandwidth running much slower than the wired backbone, wireless vendors were pulling out all of the stops to level the playing field.

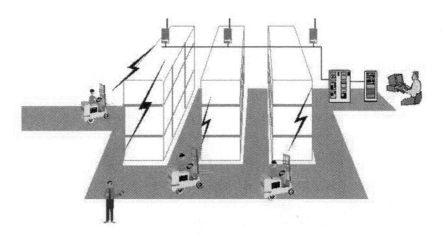

In the 1990's, data collection vendors began offering subsecond response time guarantees to satisfy the performance needs of customers. Response time—and in particular, subsecond response time—became an issue with wireless solutions as the IT teams became more involved with the technology decision. The issue that the IT staff was looking to reconcile was that the wireless media was running at less than 500 Kbps and connecting to a 10 Mbps Ethernet. While spatial reuse helped vendors meet this responsiveness, transaction density played against it. When users are spread out over a multiple cell coverage area, sporadically communicating with the network and host application, transaction times can be subsecond. The problem occurs when all of the users begin trying to communicate at the same time in the same access point coverage area. This transaction density spike was very common for a new shift of workers who were entering the work area and logging on at the same time and in the same place. Customers were unhappy because the transaction times for this particular transaction were much slower than was often "guaranteed."

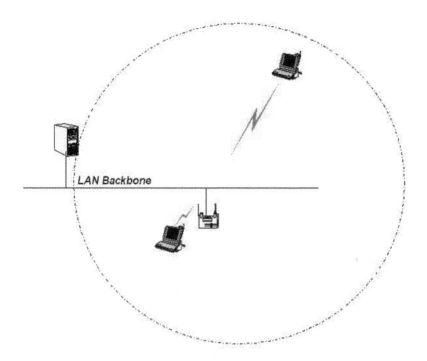

The key to success in this scenario is to understand that this slowness is only temporary with normal coverage. Another solution is to design around the problem by providing additional bandwidth (e.g., stacking access points) in the coverage area where there is significant activity. This area may be where everyone logs in before moving to their work area in a warehouse environment or where the sale team gathers when they visit the corporate office.

NEAR-FAR

Even with technology advancements and industry standards, simple problems still exist. The near-far problem is an issue with two nodes. As the problem is named, one is near the access point and the other is far away. While both radios will listen before they attempt to transmit, as part of collision dense multiple access (CDMA) protocol, the stronger signal of the nearer radio will not allow the weaker signal to get through to the access point. While the collision takes place, this issue is addressed by the collision back-off algorithm, which tells both clients to randomly pick a waiting period before retrying to assure that these two clients will not have another problem. If there are many radios near the access point, radios that are farther out in the coverage area could experience a perceivable delay because the collision could take place with two different clients after original collision, and then back off.

HIDDEN CLIENT

The hidden client problem occurs when both clients are far away from the access point. While this problem may still exist in older system UHF or 902

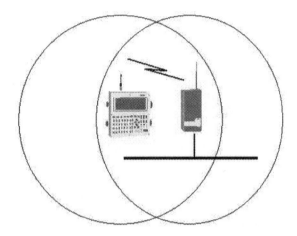

MHz wireless networks, it has been addressed in newer wireless protocols such as the IEEE 802.11 standard. The hidden client problem occurs when one client is communicating with an access point on one side of the coverage area. The access point then establishes another communication session with another client on the other side of the access point's coverage. Because of the distance between the two clients while they can both hear the access point, sometimes confusion results. One client begins sending a message to the access point, but in the middle of the message the second client listens and because it cannot hear the first client sending a message, it begins to transmit and causes confusion. In the past, this was solved as a protocol collision and both clients would retry sending their message.

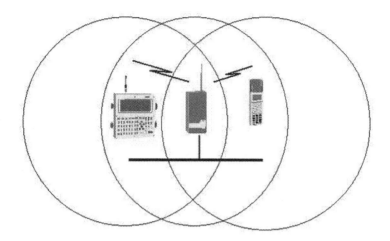

With many clients attempting to communicate and wireless bandwidth limited, the hidden client problem causes lower throughput. Having the access point send out a "busy" tone in between messages when they are communicating with a client solves this problem. This tells other clients that another client is communicating a multiple packet message.

SLEEPING CLIENT

This problem applies only to mobile clients that turn their radios off in order to conserve battery life. It occurs when the access point attempts to send a message to the client, but the client misses it because its radio is turned off. This issue was resolved by some radio vendors and also implemented in the IEEE standards committee by storing the message in the access point until it woke up and asked the access point if it had any messages while it was asleep. This added more sophistication to the access point, which was previously functioning only as a two-port bridge from the wireless media to the wired infrastructure.

MULTIPATHING

Just as light and sound bounce off of objects, so does RF. This means there can be more than one path that RF takes when going from a transmitter antenna to receiver antenna. These signals add, according to their phase relationship to produce a signal that contains the modulation of both, and has amplitude determined by how out of phase the waves are received. While multipath occurs for stationary (fixed) antennas, this variety can more easily be addressed than a mobile client that is subjected to rapid peaks and fading of the signal that occurs as the radio moves through the environment. Changing the type of antenna and the location of the antenna can eliminate multipath interference.

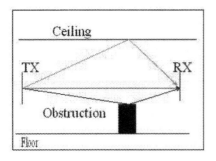 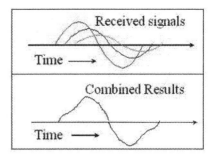

Three things can change the multipath null point.

1. Change the location of the antenna (most common).
2. Change the type of antenna, moving the main lobe of energy and affecting the reflected energy.
3. Change the frequency (this changes the wavelength, and therefore changes the points where the signals are received out of time).

Questions and Useful Tips

❖ *What is the "working path loss" for the proposed radio?*
  ➤ Like most products in the commercial marketplace, vendors make products differently and with different components. These design decisions change the performance of one vendor from another. While most vendors will have the same transmitter power, adjusting different variables (such as increasing the receiver sensitivity) will increase the coverage of the radio. Unfortunately receiver sensitivity is not on most datasheets.

❖ *Why do I hear a lot about 100 mW transmit power when the FCC allows up to 4 W in the ISM band?*
  ➤ The 100 mW is related to the restrictive nature of ETSI rather than capabilities of a radio in an FCC environment. Because most radios are designed for global shipment, the least common denominator is the ETSI regulation of 100 mW.

❖ *Is the radiation from Wi-Fi radios safe?*

➤ Under the National Environmental Policy Act of 1969, the FCC was required to evaluate the effects of RF exposure on the human body. The FCC has based it rules around guidelines put forth by the American National Standards Institute (ANSI), the National Council on Radiation Protection and Measurement (NCRPM) and the IEEE. These nongovernmental organizations have documented their thoughts on the specific absorption rate (SAR), which is the measurement of the human body's ability to absorb RF energy. This measure is not limited to radio frequency devices as it applies to everything from sunlight to cellular phone usage. The SAP limitation for work related exposure for the whole body is 400 mW/kg but for general use in uncontrolled environments it is reduced to 80 mW/kg. While 4 Watt would greatly increase the working path loss and therefore the coverage of the radio, most Wi-Fi radios use only 30 to 100 mW compared to almost 500 mW of energy being transmitted by cell phones.

❖ *Do the radio and driver allow for additional power setting beyond IEEE 802.11?*
➤ Yes. While the IEEE 802.11 specification has been set up to handle the majority of installations, some vendors have added additional power setting capabilities that increase the battery life of the mobile client. While this may be a good attribute, remember that it may also require that you use a specific vendor's access points in addition to the radio.

❖ *Can I make my entire facility one data rate using IEEE 802.11b radios instead of 11, 5.5, 2,1 Mbps?*
➤ Yes. This is an option from some manufacturers. It is important to check before purchasing a radio if this is one of the criteria needed for installation. Manufacturers with this option allow the user to set the speed of the radio through the settings in the radio driver.

❖ *What is PC card format?*
➤ "PC card" is short for PCMCIA, Personal Computer Manufacturers. The PCMCIA publishes standards for the personal computing industry. Version 2.1 provides information about the necessary connector on the end of the card that is inserted into the computer, the pin-out for the card, the physical size and power. A complete specification is available at www.pcmcia.org.

❖ *What is the maximum power that is allowed by the FCC?*
➤ The FCC allows up to 4 watts EIRP for point to multi-point applications. Most mobile clients will have between 50 mW and 100 mW for global implementations (ETSI regulations only allow 100 mW maximum) and power consumption purposes.

❖ *How do I know if I have multipath interference?*

➢ Multipath interference can be difficult to diagnose, but an experienced troubleshooter looks for conditions that are common for multi-pathing. Environmental conditions, such as metal roofs and side walls of storage buildings point strongly to multipathing—especially if you are standing within line of site of the antenna and not getting any coverage because the signals are out of phase and canceling each other, creating a null spot.

Antennas and Accessories

Overview

Understanding antenna gain and antenna patterns is key to making the most out of the coverage area with access points. The role of the antennas differs with the passage of time and the introduction of new advancements in technology. When antennas were used with licensed UHF radios, accessories (such as attenuators) were used to limit the coverage area because the energy of the signal was very strong. With 900 MHz solutions, the amount of energy was less and the role of the antenna changed to optimizing the RF coverage area because access points were expensive (costing between $2,000 and $2,500). With 2.4 GHz solutions, the amount of energy is smaller (typically 100 mW), but the cost of access points is much less ($100—$200). So the role of the antenna is less because the cost of the antenna may not justify its implementation in relation to buying another access point and using a standard di-pole antenna that ships from the manufacturer.

Basic Use

An antenna is an extension of the radio that converts high frequency (RF) signals into propagated waves in the air. The electrical energy creates fields that are emitted from antennas. These fields are called beams or lobes. Antennas can be used to mold or shape these fields into a desired coverage area. Different antennas create different shapes.

Simplifying Antenna Behavior

How antennas impact a wireless coverage area can be shown by the following analogy. The initial working path loss or amount of energy is known for a particular radio frequency based on the transmit power, or receiver sensitivity for a specific frequency and modulation.

GAIN

When a gain antenna is used, it amplifies the energy that is available, giving the impression that there is additional energy.

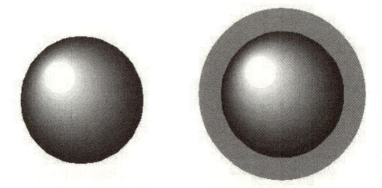

The amount of gain is determined by the type of antenna used. Additionally, there are other accessories (such as amplifiers) that can be used for injecting gain or making the amount of working path loss energy (signal strength) larger.

LOSS

Loss describes the decrease in energy (signal strength) used to propagate the radio wave. As there are a number of factors that can produce gain, there are also things that can affect the signal electrically as it travels to the antenna. The most common component of loss is the resistance of cables and connectors, which attenuates the signal by converting some of the energy to heat. Impedance mismatches in cables and connectors can also cause problems, which degrades the signal.

POLARIZATION

A radio wave is actually made up of two fields, one electrical and one magnetic. These two fields are 90° apart, or perpendicular, to each other. Polarization is important because as we pull the RF energy into a coverage pattern that is created by the antenna we select, polarization determines the orientation of the pattern.

Antennas

There are three basic antenna types that are used to get the most out of the RF energy: omni-directional, semi-directional (which includes elliptical and patch antennas) and yagi antennas.

OMNI-DIRECTIONAL (DI-POLE)

The omni-directional is the most basic antenna. It uses the gain to amplify the basic doughnut-like coverage signal of the antenna. Also called a di-pole antenna, it is simple to design and is the standard antenna included on most access points. An omni-directional antenna gets its name because it radiates its energy equally in all directions around its axis in a doughnut pattern.

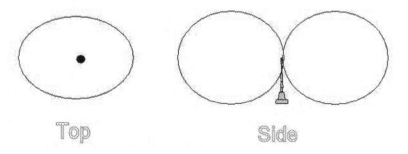

Omni-directional antennas tend not to be used because of the scatter of the RF signal. If a di-pole antenna were placed on an access point that is mounted on the ceiling, half of the energy would be radiated upward to an area where there would be no clients. If the antenna were mounted on a mobile client near the ground, half of the energy would be directed toward the floor.

Sample omni-directional antennas include the following:

➢ Di-pole antennas, which can be optionally ordered with PC card radios
➢ Omni-pillar mount antenna
➢ Omni-ground plane antenna
➢ Omni-ceiling mount antenna

Elliptical Antenna

The elliptical antenna is the best antenna in an implementer's arsenal for extending coverage. The elliptical shape is similar to an omni-directional antenna, except that the top and bottom are squashed. This extends the coverage beyond the omni-directional, lowering the access point to coverage ratio.

This "squashing" eliminates energy that would be sent into the ceiling and uses it to extend the coverage area on the horizontal axis.

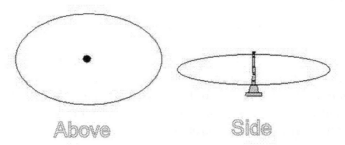

Above   Side

Usage

Omni-directional antennas are used when coverage in all directions around the horizontal axis of the antenna is required. With the ability to select the specific shape of the necessary coverage area, true omni-directional antennas are not used very often. Even in multi-story buildings, concrete floors tend to limit the signal from one floor to another, and in most cases the next floor may not be required. For small and large facilities, the elliptical antenna is the best choice.

SEMI-DIRECTIONAL

Semi-directional antennas allow implementers to "trim" the edges of a coverage area. The ability for these antennas to direct all of their energy in one direction instead of uniformly makes patch or panel antennas great for covering the outside walls of a building.

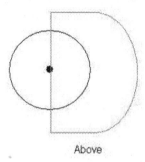

Above

Patch Antenna

The specific gain of a patch antenna is determined by the frequency of the antenna, but the coverage pattern will remain the same.
Differences in the amount of gain will determine the size of the coverage pattern.

Usage

The half circle pattern of the patch antenna has been designed to be mounted on an outside wall of the building, facing inward and radiating all of its energy in the semi-circle pattern. The use of a patch antenna occurs when coverage is being designed so that it does not extend outside the building or a designated coverage area.

YAGI ANTENNA

A yagi antenna takes the available radio energy and directs it into a thin narrow pattern. The first and very common application for a yagi antenna is building-to-building communications, where the narrow beam is used to extend the reach of the destination building. Parabolic dish or highly directional grid antennas are also good selections for building-to-building applications, and provide a narrow beam of energy that can be focused to a distance location.

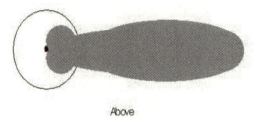

Above

A popular indoor use for directional antennas such as a yagi is facilities where there are high racks, metal shelves or radio-absorbing material (such as paper). The use of a yagi antenna can provide wireless coverage further down an aisle or narrow space in these situations, with the purpose of providing coverage down a complete aisle so that cable and power do not have to be run to the middle of the facility.

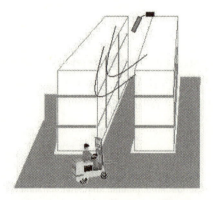

With the reduced price of access points in the market, implementers must weigh the cost of adding power and network connectivity to an additional access point versus the purchase of an external antenna, which will extend of the coverage of installed antennas.

Phased Array Antennas

Phased array antenna technology is a method of providing an intelligent antenna or set of antennas that can be used to eliminate the need for access points. Software controlling the antennas detects Wi-Fi clients in the area and adjusts the signal across the array many times per second. The system has the effect of providing a directional antenna from the phased array to each of the clients that have been detected. The goal is to create directed beams of radio waves rather than a large spherical coverage area. The cost benefit is the elimination of cabling and power necessary to install the additional access points.

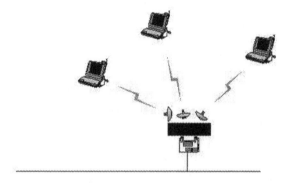

Antenna Installation and Mounting

Once an antenna has been selected, correct installation is very important. Improper installation can cause damage or destruction of the antenna, or at a minimum cause a problem that changes the coverage area and causes a coverage hole.

Antenna Mounting Options

Because there are a variety of differing environments that antennas will be mounted in, there are many different mounting options. The most popular are ceiling mount, wall mount and pillar mount. When mounting antennas, remember that many times the mounting brackets shipped with the antenna will not be the ones required to mount the antenna in your environment. An installer may need to make adjustments to the provided brackets. If adjustments are needed, remember that an antenna is not designed to be dangled by its cable but should be securely mounted.

Antenna Accessories

When it comes time to put everything together, the following accessories may be part of the final assembly for installing the antennas for their designated uses. Many of the items in this section are optional, and it is important to understand why and how different components will be used in connecting the antenna to the access point.

AMPLIFIERS

An amplifier is attached between the access point and the antenna where it boosts the electrical energy of the signal before it's converted into radio waves. Amplifiers should not be used for indoor applications, but are occasionally used for outdoor point-to-multiple or point-to-point building-to-building communications. It is key that the customer understands the EIRP of the solution, because they will be responsible for any FCC violations and subsequent fines. For example, a ski resort customer wanted to extend its LAN up to the top of the mountain for a point-of-sale application. In this case, the 100 mW access point signal was boosted for a point-to-point connection to a parabolic antenna on both ends of the connection. The wireless vendor access point allowed a second radio to be used in the access point. This second radio provided local area coverage for the facility at the top of the mountain.

ATTENUATORS

Attenuators are used to limit the coverage of an access point. They are placed between the access point and that antenna. They can be viewed as the inverse of the amplifier. Attenuators take the electrical energy from the access point and convert a portion of it to heat. They send the rest to the antenna, where it is converted to radio waves. In the past, attenuators were common because of the output power and the path loss characteristics of the frequencies that were being used. Today, attenuators can be found in application at a retail store in a mall where they are used to limit the coverage so that not just anyone can sit in the mall with a laptop and attempt to attach to an access point that has coverage outside of the building.

LIGHTNING ARRESTORS

The deployment of computers throughout many companies has made looking at potential lightning damage part of a bigger picture. Companies now address power spikes that may be caused by lightning on power or data lines before either enters the building. In the past, power surges needed to be addressed separately as power and data were installed outside of the office. Previously, this was the responsibility of the IT department in industrial settings for vertical applications. While this issue has faded to lesser importance, it is important to make sure it is addressed.

SPLITTERS

Splitters are installed after the access point, and split the signal in two for separate antennas. If a splitter is being used, it is important to understand how and why, especially with the 100 mW 2.4 GHz access point. With the lower cost of access points, it is better to install another access point than to install an amplifier on an access point, split the signal and attach two antennas. In the past, this methodology was used because of larger signal outputs, which may or may not have required an amplifier, and the different characteristics of the working path loss energy that went further, depending on the frequency deployed.

CABLES AND CONNECTORS

While the cable and connectors that connect the access point to the antenna may appear to be accessory items, they are an important part of the coverage equation. Without a low loss cable and proper connectors, the RF energy that is lost to heat as it travels to the antenna can exceed -3 dB, which is half of the original coverage area. Sloppy connectors and the wrong cable can easily exceed—6 dBm loss, or three quarters of the original energy available to provide coverage to a particular area.

Antenna Installation

Once the RF energy has reached the antenna, it is very important to have proper installation of the antennas in a wireless LAN. An improper installation can lead to poor performance, damage to the equipment and, in some cases, personal injury. In order to get good performance when installing antennas, it is important to use the correct antenna and to orient and align it properly.

APPROPRIATE USE

Mixing and matching antennas is not good, because antennas tend to be manufactured for specific uses. Therefore, it is important to use indoor antennas inside of buildings and outdoor antennas outside of them. Keeping it simple can prevent problems if troubleshooting is necessary. Outdoor antennas tend to be sealed to prevent water from entering the element area, and are made of the appropriate materials to withstand the outdoor weather. If there are questions about the antenna being specified, it should be asked at the time the site survey report is received and/or reviewed. If changes are needed because the initial assumptions associated with the site survey have changed, it may be best to have that portion of the site survey redone rather than risk the problems associated with a poor installation.

ORIENTATION AND ALIGNMENT

Antenna orientation determines the polarization. Proper orientation is necessary to get the results associated with the site survey. Alignment applies typically to outdoor installations in building-to-building solutions where the narrow beam of the radio signal needs to be able to be captured by the corresponding highly directional antenna. It is important for all antenna installations, including those installed indoors.

Antenna Installation Safety

Antennas are an extension of the wireless network but like other electrical devices, they can be dangerous to implement or operate. It is recommended that if there is a problem with a remote or external antenna that you use a wireless professional for the installation. While the operation of antennas is straightforward, there are a number of things that can decrease the performance, especially related to outdoor building-to-building antennas (such as parabolic or grid antennas) that in addition to being very sensitive are also very expensive.

DO NOT TOUCH

While it may look interesting, never touch a high-gain antenna with any part of your body while it is attached to an access point that is plugged in. The FCC allows very high amounts of energy to be transmitted, especially in building-to-building links. Either touching or putting any part of your body in the radio path in the 2.4 GHz range is the equivalent of putting your body in a microwave oven, which also operates in the 2.4 GHz range.

METAL OBSTRUCTIONS

Keep antennas away from metal obstructions. For outdoor installations, this includes heating and air ducts or any metal that may be on the roof of the building. For indoor installations this includes large ceiling trusses, ducts or metal ceilings or walls because the metal will reflect the signal and cause multipathing.

Questions and Useful Tips

❖ *What type of antenna does the client radio have? Is it a gain antenna?*
  ➤ This is important, because some radios are designed to have a patch, where the signal is radiating in one direction. Even though all of the products that may be concerned may have the same radio from the same vendor, the installation of the radio can make all of the difference in coverage and performance. If a PC card radio with a patch antenna is installed upside down in the manufacturing process (as happens occasionally), all of the energy will be radiated into the ground and not upwards toward the access points. This mistake can cause a large number of retries or coverage holes (where there is no communication), even though the site survey says that the coverage is good. The same especially holds true to vendors who embed radios into their mobile computers where it is difficult to see if the radio is installed upside down. Additionally, any sealing or components sitting on top of the radio antenna can affect the performance. The best answer is a client radio with an omni-directional pattern. It is important to understand the antenna pattern of the client device.
❖ *When should I see a splitter attached to my antenna?*
  ➤ It depends. For UHF or even 900 MHz solutions, splitters are common because there is so much working path energy that a splitter allows the energy to be redirected, and therefore expands the coverage. With the low cost and smaller working path energy (coverage) of 2.4 GHz access points, there is no need for splitters. In a 2.4 GHz installation, a splitter is just another point of failure.
❖ *My site survey has an attenuator listed as part of the recommended components. Why?*

> ➢ Attenuators are used to bleed the working path energy off into heat before it reaches the antenna. This is typically done with radio solutions that have a lot of energy, such as UHF or 900 MHz configurations, but can be done with any radio where the site survey technician is looking to limit the coverage. Usually limiting the coverage area is a request that is made by the customer. Reasons for limiting the coverage could include that the facility is located in a mall or in an office building with other offices nearby. In this case, the attenuator reduces the coverage area so that the signal does not permeate outside of the requested coverage area.

❖ *When is an amplifier used?*
> ➢ Amplifiers are typically used in point-to-point wireless communications where a gain antenna does not provide enough signal for reliable communications. It is important to request a copy of the EIRP calculations from anyone who recommends an amplifier, because boosting the output power to the antenna can cause it to exceed regulations, which can lead to fines from the FCC.

❖ *Should I use a lightning arrestor on each access point?*
> ➢ This question should be researched with the maintenance or facilities staff. The question should be rephrased to ask whether the electrical system has sufficient protection to handle an electrical power surge, whether the surge is caused by a lightning strike or a generator switchover. Twenty years ago, many of the places where wireless was being installed did not have surge protection. But with the proliferation of desktop computers, companies have realized the need to protect all of their electrical components, not just those associated with the wireless solution.

❖ *Should I adjust the antenna on an access point?*
> ➢ It depends. The rule of thumb is that if the antenna is remote or external and not directly attached to the access point, it should be adjusted or changed by a wireless professional. This is because external or remote antennas are used for a specific purpose, and without understanding that purpose any adjustments could cause problems in the coverage or performance. This rule does not typically apply to office access points that have small wip antennas attached that may have been bumped and need to be resituated.

Site Surveys

Overview

A site survey is a study of the environment where wireless service will be provided. A good site survey will contain many questions. The answers to these questions will determine the number and placement of access points, which will formulate the wireless coverage and be the bridge from the wireless domain to the wired infrastructure. Whether it is performed by the internal personnel or by an external service provider, a site survey is needed to assure reliable wireless communications.

Through a set of task-by-task processes, the surveyor discovers the RF behavior, coverage and interference and determines the proper hardware placement of the access point(s) in the facility. Many issues can arise that prevent the RF signal from reaching certain parts of the facility that need to be covered. While the tools provided by many radio vendors make doing a site survey easier, doing a site survey without understanding the business application which will be using the wireless domain is invited failure. This section provides a guideline for what to expect from an internal or external site survey, whether it is the methodology used for the site survey or questions to ask that need to be included in final report

Evaluating Site Survey Service Providers

Before selecting an external site survey provider, be aware that the provider should be able to provide you with a procedure of how they will be conducting the site survey. This should include the specific methodology that they will be using to conduct the survey, a set of questions concerning your environment and an example of a site survey report. Additionally, they should let you know how many surveys the company has completed and provide a list of reference accounts that you can call.

Preparing for the Site Survey

The planning of a wireless LAN involves collecting information and making decisions. Understanding the basic business fundamentals that are driving the wireless implementation can help in the decision making process. For example, if high throughput is needed for a heavily traveled area, this may affect the channels used in adjacent coverage areas.

You should also be aware of the people who are available to answer your questions and any other technical resources. The three most important people for a successful wireless installation will be the facilities manager, the network manager and the operations manager. The facilities manager (or similar position) will assist in providing the blueprints for the facility as well as AC power for the access points once the location has been determined. The network manager will be aware of cabling and host related issues. It will also be important to understand the current network scheme while working together to assure IP addresses are assigned as well as the security policy for the facility. The operations manager will be able to answer questions on how the wireless network will be used which will provide answers to the necessary throughput in any specific location as well as roaming requirements.

The following information should be collected as part of a pre-site survey questionnaire. Typically, this can be done by an email is the provider sends to the site or with a phone call. It is upfront work to determine any considerations that would help provide the best use of time once the site survey signal and coverage mapping has started.

Area/Facilities Analysis

In what kind of area will the wireless network be installed? This basic question opens the door to many questions, because an outside open area requires a different site survey than an indoor facility. A site survey for a college campus is different from one for a small carpeted office with low ceilings and ten potential users or from a 1 million square foot manufacturing facility; each may require different tools to complete the site survey with over 100 simultaneous users. Typically, this is just the leaping point as each implementation has a set of questions that needs to be answered.

Existing Networks

Is there already a network (wired or wireless) installed? Some facilities will have a wired network, such as Ethernet, in place that is being used for office applications, whereas a new warehouse may have no communication infra-structure at all. If there is a wireless network, there is a plethora of information that must be gathered:

- ➤ Frequency installed
  - o UHF, if so what frequency
  - o 900 MHz
  - o 2.4 GHz
- ➤ Vendor installed
- ➤ Number of users
- ➤ Application using this wireless network
- ➤ Other wireless equipment (such as 900 MHz phones or industrial tags)
- ➤ Operating Systems used on the network
- ➤ Anticipated number of users (today and in the future)
- ➤ Network protocols used
  - o So that others may be filtered at the access point
- ➤ Security policies
  - o Will 802.1x be used?
  - o What authentication mechanism?
  - o What authorization mechanism?
  - o VPN
  - o VLAN
  - o Remote dial-up
- ➤ Network diagram
  - o Will wireless be a single segment implementation? Separate from the enterprise infrastructure.
  - o Where are the routers?
  - o Is the network switched?
  - o Is the network bridged?
- ➤ Network Naming convention
  - o Static IP address
  - o DHCP
  - o Access Points—proxy naming convention for access points, typi-cally the location so they can be found
- ➤ Wiring closet location

OUTSIDE USAGE

There are special requirements for equipment that is used outside. Typically, this would be for building-to-building communications (either point-to-point or point-to-multiple) and can consist of campus coverage for mobile students, yard coverage for trucks being moved for staging or outside-the-dock coverage for shipping and receiving applications. In all cases, the access point will be outside. In addition to the weather, we will also address security. Security is an issue because a rooftop mounted access point needs only to be disconnected and attached to a laptop for an intruder to have wired access to the network.

In an outdoor environment, a NEMA (National Equipment Manufacturer's Association) compliant enclosure will be used. NEMA certifies enclosures are capable of performing certain tasks such as being weather proof (which is NEMA 3).

If the wireless coverage will be outside, potential obstructions such as trees, vehicles and buildings need to be noted on the site survey.

PURPOSE AND BUSINESS REQUIREMENTS

What is the purpose of the wireless LAN? What are the business requirements?

The number of devices that will be used, the amount of data per device and the expected response time can be answered by understanding the business requirements. IEEE 802.11 radios can perform at 1, 2, 5.5 and 11 Mbps. While one radio provides that performance, each throughput has a different coverage pattern, with a 1 Mbps coverage footprint being much larger than an 11 Mbps network.

If there are only five or six clients moving a small amount of data with no plans to upgrade, providing 11 Mbps throughout the facility is only adding the cost of purchasing and installing access points for capacity that will not be used.

COMMUNICATE THROUGHPUT EXPECTATIONS

If it can be determined that there are areas of high transaction density, additional access points can be cascaded to provide more wireless bandwidth to the specific area. It is important that everyone understand the throughput expectations upfront so that additional throughput can be designed into the solution. This expectation can drastically change the number of access points or even the recommended frequency of operation. There are several ways that increased throughput can be achieved, whether it is stacking the access points or merely overlapping them in high traffic areas.

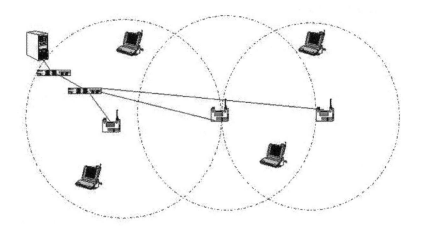

Stacking Coverage

Stacking coverage involves putting two or more access points in the same coverage area on different channels. In essence, the multiple coverage areas are "stacked" one on top of another. This allows clients to attach to one of up to three different access points in the same coverage area and provides additional access to the network or throughput. The biggest issue with stacking is that in an IEEE environment, there are only three non-overlapping coverage areas. So if the stacked coverage cell is integrated into a larger coverage area, there is the potential for adjacent interference.

Overlapping Coverage

Overlapping coverage uses multiple access points, but instead of stacking them in close proximity in the same coverage area, they are separated. This allows the access points to be used for additional coverage and throughput, if necessary, but also provides redundancy for part of one or more other coverage areas in the event of an access point failure. Due to the high cost of not being able to use the wireless application, companies with mission critical applications will provide overlapping coverage so that a mobile client will always have minimally 2 access points that they can hear and roam to as needed.

Site Survey Necessities

The following is a guideline for equipment that is needed to perform a successful site survey.

A digital camera—This is very important because it provides specific visual documentation of the facility. Little is left to interpretation when a digital picture is provided of where the access point is going to be placed.

Battery powered access point—While power will be provided for the permanent installation of the access point, it is a requirement that the access point be tested in the location in which it will ultimately be mounted and providing coverage. **Note that a laptop functioning as an access point is not a substitute for the equipment that will be installed; it is difficult to attach remote antennas to laptop radios.**

Different antennas—A site survey technician should have several types of antennas to use, depending on the environment. At a minimum, the technician should have an elliptical and a patch antenna. Unless the coverage area is a single cell in an office building, an elliptical gain antenna can increase the coverage by ~35-50% over the standard di-pole antenna supplied by the vendor. Depending on the answers to the pre-site survey questions, a yagi antenna may also be needed to measure coverage in certain scenarios. The goal is to have all of tools necessary to perform the task the first time and minimize the number of times required to return to complete the survey.

Site schematics—1/4th or 1/8th size print—These mark the location of the coverage boundary and show the location of the access points.

Client (fixed or mobile)—Whether the wireless client will be roaming through the wireless coverage transferring data or staying in the same location, it is important to the client, if possible, for the site survey. This provides the most realistic coverage scenario.

Tape or chalk—These mark coverage boundary during the survey process.

Distance wheel or tape measure—These measure distances from access points or walls for documentation on the schematic.

Spectrum analyzer—This is special purpose and optional. A spectrum analyzer will be needed if other networks were indicated as answers to pre-site survey questions.

Network analyzer—This equipment is optional.

Site Survey Approaches and Methodologies

There are several approaches and methodologies that can be used to conduct a site survey. The most common indoor methodology is a boundary approach, which can be applied either to a data rate site survey or a coverage site survey. The only difference between the two is that a data rate site survey is guaranteeing a minimum data rate for the coverage area. For some applications, 11 Mbps data rate (802.11b) or 54 Mbps (802.11g) is needed throughout the coverage area to service the application. These site survey will have more access points than a coverage site survey because the access point boundary is documented when the radio rate shifts from 11 Mbps to 5.5 Mbps, instead of when the radio can no longer communicate to the access point.

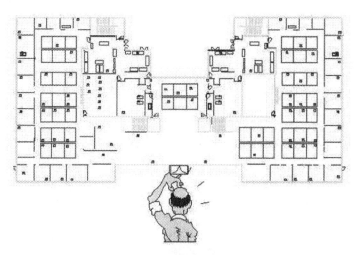

In most applications, coverage at any throughput will be the requested approach, but it is always good to make sure so that the expectations between the customer and the site survey technician are the same. Even though coverage may be the intent of the site survey, it is always good to note the data rate boundaries as part of the data-gathering phase of the survey.

In addition to access point placement, coverage and data rate boundaries, the following items should be located on the blueprint that has been provided:

- ➢ All AC power outlets and grounding points
- ➢ Wiring closets
- ➢ Computer room
- ➢ Wired network connections
- ➢ Elevation requirements for access point placement, e.g., ladders or lifts

> ➢ Potential obstructions such as fire doors, kitchen areas, elevators, low ceilings

THE BOUNDARY APPROACH

The basic premise of the boundary approach is to start at the edge of the coverage area, typically a corner of a building. By placing the access point here and walking away or into the potential coverage we can be assured of coverage on this edge. When the signal has been stretched to the edge, mark this spot.

Now switch the access point and the client. There should be no difference in the signal. Having the access point mounted away from the wall is like having the round signature of an omni-directional antenna or elliptical antenna fit the square peg of the corner of the building. It is important to test the corner to assure that there are no dead spots. Proper placement is important when using an omni-directional or elliptical antenna because it may result in unused signal propagating outside the building.

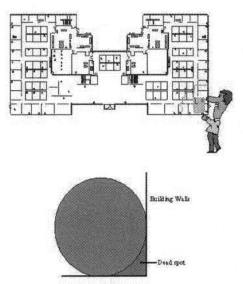

Once this initial access point has been properly placed, the coverage that it provides should be marked on the schematic and a picture taken with the digital camera for the recommended location. While not necessary, it is recommended that colored markers or pens be used to mark the coverage area on the schematic. This way, there is no confusion in understanding the specific coverage of a single access point. This is especially important for sites where there is overlapping coverage. The digital picture will be placed in the final site survey report and leaves little doubt to the specific location that has been tested. The site survey technician will determine the spot of the next access point by placing it on the coverage boundary of the previously placed access point.

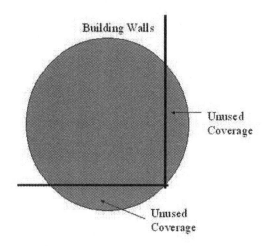

Again, after stretching the coverage, the access point and the client are switched. Because there are many points on the coverage boundary that can be used, no two site surveys will be the same. All site survey technicians should be able to explain why they placed access points in their locations, usually for mounting reasons, network cabling requirements (distance from the hub/switch) and/or the amount of overlapping coverage that they are providing.

After repeating this process, the site survey will be documented and completed. Be prepared to move access points around and change the coverage area to assure the optimum coverage pattern. By the time the site survey is done, the blueprint should be well marked up with coverage and data rate information for each access point.

VERIFICATION TESTING

There are several ways that information being provided can be verified. The easiest and the most common verification is for the site survey technician to take signal to noise ratio readings and data rate readings at various points in the coverage cell when he or she is documenting the coverage.

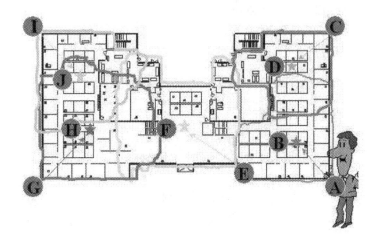

DATA RATE GUARANTEE

If a specific data rate has been specified as the minimum data rate, such as 5.5 Mbps or 11 Mbps, the site survey company should be able to guarantee their work. This guarantee will state that if there is sub-standard performance, they will fix it at no charge to the customer. When this type of guarantee is requested, it is important to review and understand the site survey recommendations because the number of access points may be overkill to assure that the guarantee is met.

COVERAGE GUARANTEE

A coverage guarantee should be standard with any site survey to assure the work has been completed in a quality manner. While most people will ask if a coverage guarantee is offered, it is important to read, upfront, what kind of guarantee is being offered. If a wireless network is installed in an office environment and cubicle walls are changed, it will affect the reflection and absorption of the signal and may cause a dead spot. The coverage guarantee more than likely will not cover the site survey because of the changes. In industrial environments, this may apply to racking being moved or product being added. Many site survey companies recommend that the site survey be completed when all possible product or people are in place so that the coverage is maximized. This way, if items are taken away, there is no problem.

READING THE REPORT

A sample copy of a site survey report has been included in the appendix, but there are no standards that define how a site survey report should be formatted. The following headings are suggested; it is important to realize that all of the information in the report makes implementing and maintaining the wireless network much easier. The site survey report is not limited to the information proposed in the example report but should be considered a minimum. Be sure to ask questions when the report is delivered if information is not contained in the final copy.

Purpose and Business Requirements

The site survey should include all contact information for both the site survey company and the customer. This section will typically restate the goals of the site survey, based on the questions that have been asked by the technician (including areas of requested coverage and usage intent, such as applications and number of users).

Methodology

It is important to understand how the site survey was conducted. This helps to explain why decisions were made. Typically, no two site surveys will be exactly the same, so understanding how the site survey was conducted and therefore, the assumptions, is important.

Coverage Areas

The schematic of the facility should contain documentation of the coverage cells. If there were special needs, such as overlapping coverage in a certain area or stocked access points to increase the throughput, it should be noted on the schematics (which should be included in the report). This part of the document is essentially showing the work and/or work in progress as the coverage map was development by the site survey technician.

Throughput

Throughput measurements that were made during the site survey should be noted on the schematic also. If possible, screen shots from the site survey tool should be included only because there are different site survey tools and the information that is request may be displayed differently. Again, throughput measurement shows the work being completed by the site survey technician and adds validity to the survey should there be any questions.

Interference

There should be details on any interference that was found, as well as the changes in coverage patterns associated with obstructions or obstacles.

Problem Areas

Any problem areas or issues should be documented. This section, or one like it, should include areas of concern for the wireless installation. This section may include the location of a freezer, microwave or elevator shaft that may cause interference during the operation of the wireless network.

Equipment Drawing

An equipment drawing should reference the blue prints that have been marked up with the coverage areas delineated. The equipment drawing will typically be a network diagram that is completed in a commercial software package such as Visio. Each component should have the following minimum information:

> The equipment drawing should include each access point with an identifier or name. This nomenclature can be discussed with the IT team or a generic identifier can be used for the purposes of the site survey report.

  o Where and how should each access point be mounted? There should be a digital picture of the location with a description of how it is mounted and on what channel it operates.

  o What is the type of antenna that will be used? Where will it be pointing? What are the cables that will be used to connect it to the access point?

  o What kind of power is needed, and how will it be provided?

  o How will data be provided to the unit?

Questions and Useful Tips

❖ *Does the company I buy the equipment from have to do the site survey?*

> If you are working with a company on the purchase of wireless equipment, it is important to know if they will be doing the site survey or if they will have a third party do the survey. Many distributors and

resellers outsource their site survey work. While many of the companies that do site surveys as part of their service do a good job, it is
important to understand how issues will be resolved if there is a problem or questions regarding the site survey and the performance of the
equipment that was recommended.

❖ *Who will do throughput testing?*
  ➢ Part of the information that should be asked as part of the site survey
    is the number of users and the type of application. This allows the site
    survey technician to understand the throughput needs. Once the
    throughput requirements are understood and agreed to by both par-
    ties, it is important to note in the site survey report how it was tested.
    Many site survey companies will test the throughput with a single
    client radio in the coverage area. If throughput is very important to
    the success of the application, it should be asked that a thorough
    throughput test be conducted. If this is anticipated, it should be
    reviewed upfront with the site survey company, as some companies do
    not have the testing equipment or capability. This typically will involve
    setting up a server and generating the amount of anticipated traffic in
    the coverage cell and measuring the throughput.

❖ *Are there any existing wireless LANs in use or near the facility?*
  ➢ Existing LANs can be a problem with attempting to complete a new
    survey, especially if the existing LANs cannot be turned off during the
    survey. Disabling the existing LAN may not be possible, because it is
    currently being used for production operations or the interfering
    wireless LAN may be part of a solution that is being used by another
    company. If the problem is production line related, usually the site
    survey can be scheduled for non-production hours.

❖ *Are there future plans for additional applications or users using wireless communications in this facility?*
  ➢ This question looks at the bigger picture. Sometimes an application
    such as shipping or receiving gets approval, which will require mobil-
    ity and therefore the installation of a wireless LAN. If additional appli-
    cations or more users will be added, it is best to take that into
    consideration at the time of the site survey. This additional step can
    make sure that the entire facility is covered for 11 Mbps if 2.4 GHz is
    used.

❖ *Are there any common sources of RF interference?*
  ➢ New installation should use 2.4 GHz or 5 GHz frequencies unless
    there is a special purpose application. Because both of these bands are
    in the ISM band and unlicensed, there is a potential for interference.

In the 2.4 GHz band, common interference sources include break room microwave ovens and wireless garage door openers. Other equipment that should be considered includes the following:

- Freezers
- Cordless phones
- Baby monitors
- Radiology equipment in medical facilities
- Cellular towers
- Radio station towers
- Electricity transmission lines

❖ *Are there other objects that can cause coverage problems?*

➢ Yes, there are also obstacles that can cause signal loss. Common sources of interference are items that will reflect the signal, such as the following:

- Metal mesh cubicles
- Metal mesh windows
- Metal window blinds
- Fire doors
- Cement walls
- Electrical transformers
- Metal studded walls

There are also items that will absorb signal, such as the following:

- Paper
- Cardboard

❖ *Is this a multi-tenant building?*

➢ For multi-tenant buildings, it is possible that another company may have a wireless network installed that could impact the site survey. This is found most often in wireless networks are installed as extensions of office networks. If the coverage of another installation is causing problems, there are several ways to resolve the problem. Because the company may not realize that their wireless network extends into your building or onto your floor, they may attenuate it primarily for security reasons. Depending on the size of the facility, the site survey technician may simply be able to select a different channel for the new installation. Because the existing coverage extends into the proposed coverage area, we need to review rogue access point security measures. There are some software solutions that can be added onto the wireless network that will prevent the wireless clients of the proposed wireless network from attaching to anything other than defined access points.

This will eliminate any security issues. This measure, in addition to having the site survey technician raise the signal-to-noise ratio of the proposed network, will provide a good solution. Increasing the signal to noise ratio means that the proposed network will have a stronger signal and the clients will not roam to the other network because of a stronger radio signal strength indicator (RSSI).

❖ *What should I know about the equipment suggested by the site survey vendor?*
  ➢ The site survey equipment should include a complete description of the equipment necessary to implement the site survey as it was performed. It is important to ask **upfront** how the equipment will be documented. Some site survey companies will include only their own internal equipment descriptions and part numbers as part of the site survey results. When they do this, they are attempting to make you use them for purchasing the equipment as well as doing the installation of the equipment. While you may elect to do this, it should be because the company meets your selection requirements to do this, not because they did the site survey and you are locked into them or have to do another site survey. **It is important to clarify this as part of the quote before the site survey.** One method of working through this issue is to ask the site survey company to recommend three different vendors' equipment for the major components (such as access points).

❖ *What kind of due diligence should be done?*
  ➢ Prior to assigning the work to a company, be sure to ask for references and (at a minimum) an example copy of a completed site survey report. If they note that the information is proprietary to the specific customer, ask to see the sample template that is used and refer to the sample provided to assure that all of the necessary information is included in the report. This will help assure that there are no wrong expectations between what is expected and the deliverable.

❖ *The site survey report recommends a remote antenna. Is this OK?*
  ➢ Remote antennas are the best way to expand the coverage of an access point with minimal expense. While another access point may be added in a different, the cost of running power and Ethernet cable to additional locations or another hub on the network in the facility adds costs to the implementation. The important things to consider about remote antennas are making sure that site survey was conducted with the antenna that is being recommended and assuring the cable (including cable connections) are low loss. It is important that all of the energy that we need for the wireless coverage makes it to the access point and is not leaked out of the cable or cable connections. It is also

important to understand that the length of the cable should be part of the site survey results. Sometimes the installation company will supply their own cable and terminate it during installation. If this occurs, it is important that it is tested because an improper termination can lead to a non-functioning access point.

❖ *Is it OK to split the signal from an access point?*

  ➢ For IEEE 802.11, .11b/g and .11a solutions the answer is no, there should be no reason to split the signal from a single access point. In the past, splitting the signal from an access point was a way to increase coverage using the abundant link margin. This was acceptable because the signal power was much higher for 900 MHz or UHF radios and the cost of the access points was very expensive. In the 2.4 GHz band, most signals are from 50 mW to 100 mW, which are $1/10^{th}$ to $1/20^{th}$ of other radio signals and the costs have come down significantly. The problem occurs most commonly when experienced site survey technicians combine their experience from one radio band to another. Because access points were very expensive, this technique actually saved customers money by having fewer access points to install. Today, this is not effective. The only thing that should be used to increase the coverage of the access point is a gain antenna.

Wireless Devices

Overview

The kinds of devices that will be part of the wireless solution will depend on the application and where it will be installed. While the principles discussed apply to all solutions, the specific devices will vary. For example, a residential gateway may be used in a home or small office installation where a single network contact can be used instead of access points (which act as bridges to the wired infrastructure). For this type of application, PC card radios are great for laptop computers. But they may not be the solution for a workstation; they may not even be possible with older workstations not equipped with PC card slots. While the radio in the client is the most visible component of a wireless solution, another common component of the infrastructure is an access point, or *AP*. Access points and PC card radios have become the core components for wireless solutions over the last three to five years with the advent of the IEEE 802.11 standard.

Access Points

Today's access point is much different from some of the equipment that is still installed and continues to operate in businesses throughout the world. In the past, access points were known as base stations or transceivers, depending on which vendor's equipment was being installed. These base stations were not attached to an Ethernet network, but were installed in hub and spoke configurations as wired networks continued to develop into today's Ethernet.

Hub and Spoke versus Network Attach

The first wireless networks were hub and spoke architectures where "base stations" connected to controllers. The cabling was usually RS-232, RS-422 or RS-485. Some UHF installations may still be installed in single base station configurations or hub and spoke architectures. In hub and spoke architectures, a controller was the intelligence for the entire wireless network because wireless communications (whether over the air or on the wire) were proprietary. Controllers controlled the communication to the host application as well to the base stations. Controllers typically supported up to eight base stations, but could be extended if needed. Usually eight was more than enough because the radios being used were UHF, and therefore provided over 750,000 square feet of coverage with a single base station.

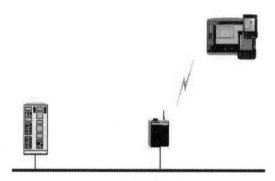

In the early to mid 1990's, the wireless industry began providing Ethernet connectivity to base stations. This connectivity and specifically 10BaseT is the de facto standard today. In the mid 1990's, the nomenclature also changed as base stations and transceivers became known as access points, in reference to the point of access to the wired network from the wireless media. In essence, access points functioned as two-port translational bridges, which translated the physical media from the wireless protocol to the wired protocol. As the market for access points has developed, vendors have begun to differentiate their products by the number of features beyond the basic standard functionality that is included in the access points. The market play is that with more intelligence in the access point, it can be sold at a higher price. The result is access point prices ranging from $200 to $2500.

DUMB ACCESS POINTS TO INTELLIGENT NETWORK APPLIANCE

As access points have become a commodity item, the price has dropped to a couple of hundred dollars. In order to maintain value add, vendors have taken enterprise functionality (such as network management or device management) that was traditionally in the access point and added it to a network appliance (such as a bridge or a switch). This configuration takes the hub and spoke network configuration and replaces the controller functionality (which interfaced with an application on a dedicated host platform) with switching or bridging functionality as an interface to the rest of the network—and therefore any application on the network.

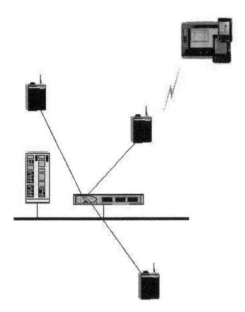

Wireless Residential Gateway

A wireless residential gateway is a device that connects a small number of wireless devices to the Internet. This type of gateway product, which minimally includes a DHCP server and a firewall, also has a radio integrated into it and is intended for use in the home. There are two configurations of residential gateways: one with a radio integrated and a second with ports that allow one or more access points to be attached. Extra ports may also allow devices to be wired directly into the gateway. Internet connectivity may include cable or DSL modems but may also accommodate analog dial-up modem capability. Connectivity may also be integrated into the residential gateway or may be provided by a separate device.

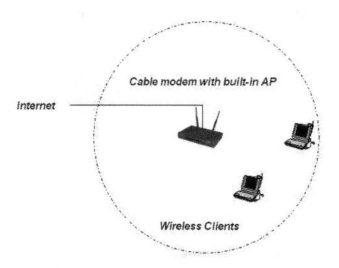

INTELLIGENT ACCESS POINTS

Intelligent access points are devices that have traditional access point capabilities and function as stand alone devices on the network. These devices are capable of being wireless bridges and repeaters in conjunction with the standard access point functionality.

MODES OF OPERATION FOR INTELLIGENT ACCESS POINTS

Access points communicate with their wireless clients, network components and other access points. The communication can be classified as access point, wired, bridging and repeating.

Basic Access Point

This is the normal functionality for an access point. Under most circumstances, it would called "bridging," because the sole purpose in this capacity is to be a two-port bridge—converting the wireless communication to the wired media. The confusion stems from similar terminology for wireless bridging, which will also be discussed. This functionality may also be known as "basic" or "root mode" capability.

In this mode, the access point is connected to the wired network (typically Ethernet) and communicates to wireless clients. It may exist as a single access point (providing all of the coverage) or work in conjunction with other access points to provide the necessary coverage. If there is more than one access point, they will communicate via the wired network to exchange information about mobile clients that have roamed from one coverage area to another.

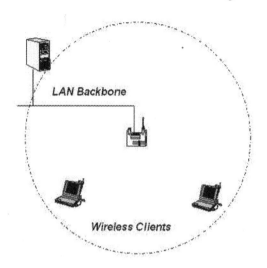

It is important to note that inter-access point communications are vendor specific and are not currently governed by standards. This is an Inter-Access Point Protocol that is currently being discussed but has not been ratified. This means that access points need to be from a single vendor. This does not apply to client radios, because their communications (when appropriate IEEE 802.11 a/b/g radios are used) are governed by the standard.

Wireless Repeating

Wireless repeating is the ability to extend the network without installing additional cabling. This functionality is typically used in areas where wiring cannot be installed (such as historic buildings, hazardous areas or areas that need temporary coverage).

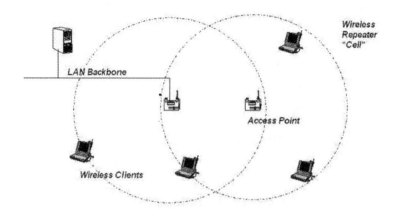

As part of the IEEE 802.11 standard, wireless bridging is implemented using the wireless distribution system (WDS) functionality. This can be implemented either with a single direct sequence radio or two radios, which may be direct sequence or frequency hopping. In the single radio mode, a second access point is powered on so that it can hear the access point connected to the wired network. This produces approximately 50% overlapping coverage, but the key is that it allows the access points to communicate to one another to exchange information (such as client roaming) via the wireless link, instead of the normally available wired link. In a two-radio implementation, one radio is used for communicating with the wired access point and the second radio is used to communicate with the mobile clients in the coverage area.

In addition to being functionally required for some installations, wireless repeating is a great temporary fit for an area that has a dead spot or no coverage, situations that may have been created after the site survey for a variety of scenarios (such as moved inventory or walls).

Wireless Bridging

Wireless bridging is a function that is usually associated with building-to-building communications, because wireless bridging usually connects two wired segments that can function as a single segment. In a single facility, it is easier to run cable to the new area and install basic access points. This is more difficult if the new area is on the other side of the railroad tracks or street.

Wireless bridges have been marketed as separate products that include basic access point functionality plus bridging logic. This additional bridging logic usually consists of filters and proxy capabilities that optimize the wireless link, because a basic network bridge would multi-cast and uni-cast messages; this is now an option with the wireless bridge set-up. Additionally, the wireless bridging can be set up to limit messages for the addresses that it has on its side of link. This is very similar to routing functionality, but again is used to optimize the wireless communication link (which in the past has been slower than its wired counterpart).

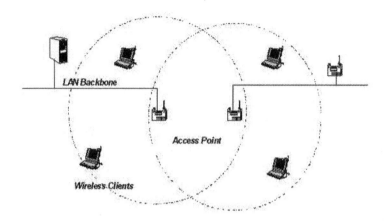

Wireless bridging can be very helpful in extending the wired network cable, but exercise caution in using this as part of the network design. The biggest concern is the introduction of a network storm caused by a loop that allows the Ethernet packets to circle back from one wired segment to another. This problem arises only for wireless bridging solutions where mobile client connectivity, and therefore, additional access points are installed on either side of the wireless bridge.

This type of problem usually occurs in a wireless installation where the environment changes after the site survey is completed. Environmental changes include events such as moving cubicle walls, opening sliding walls or moving large amounts of inventory that may have been absorbing the signal during the survey. The biggest problem with this is that if the problem is occurring, for example, in a warehouse where boxes of inventory are constantly moving, these network storms may be intermittent because the bridging loop may be connected when inventory is not in a certain location.

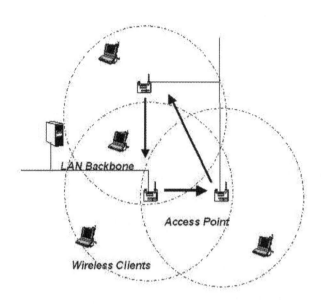

Point to Point Bridging/Routing

Wireless point to point or point to multipoint bridging has become a secondary market in wireless communications, often commanding a premium over normal access points because of the business problem it solves. While vendors continue to add functionality to provide differentiation, simple bridging can be done either by a special purpose bridge or an access point with the proper antenna. Either way, wireless bridging/routing is used to provide a communication link from one point to another, and does so because cabling is difficult to install.

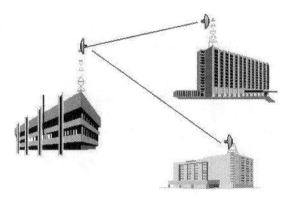

A typical example involves two buildings separated by a road or railroad tracks where there is not a conduit between the buildings that can be used to extend the wired network.. In this case, wireless bridging/routing can be very cost effective to deploy in relation to the alternative. In point-to-point configurations, the configuration contains two wireless bridges/routers. For 802.11 solutions, timing parameters prohibit a wireless bridge to remote client configuration to be used for distances greater than one mile, so make sure that two wireless bridges/routers are used and that one end is not a wireless client with a remote antenna. Additionally, it is important to understand how much data is being passed over the wireless link.

The difference between a wireless bridge and a wireless router is essentially the same as in the wired networking environment. Wireless bridges pass everything that is not filtered, including broadcast messages, multi-cast messages and proprietary messages. Wireless routers, however, pass only messages intended for the other side of the link. There can be issues where the point-to-point bridge is configured as a router; some vendors do not support IP frames with VLAN tags in routed environments. This means that the wireless link needs to be set up for bridging, which will transmit all traffic instead of only the traffic intended for points on the other side of the wireless link.

If the wireless link is intended to span long distances (five to ten miles), line of sight (LOS) and any obstruction in the 1st Fresnel zone from one antenna to another will be factors in determining the communication capability. The Fresnel zone is an elliptical area around the direct LOS that can introduce signal interference if blocked. It is important for planning purposes that no more 20-40% of the 1st Fresnel zone be blocked. Loss due to Fresnel zone obstruction can range from 6 dB to approximately 20 dB for a path having visual LOS, but full obstruction of the 1st Fresnel zone radius at only one point along the path. A knife-edge obstruction would exhibit loss closer to 6 dB, while a smooth sphere obstruction would be closer to 20 dB. Because the Fresnel zone is a concentric radius around the antenna centerline beam, it must be cleared in all directions around the beam, including above, below, and on all sides. The site survey provider or systems implementer should discuss the Fresnel zone and provide information on any blockage that exists as part of the site survey report. In evaluating the opportunity, LOS disappears after 16 miles due to the curvature of the earth.

Point to Multi-point Bridging/Routing

Point to multi-point bridging/routing has the same issues as point-to-point, except that there are multiple wireless communication paths that must adhere to the rules.

ACCESS POINT OPTIONS

In addition to varying software functionality, access points will have different physical characteristics that may affect the installation. If the site survey calls for an elliptical antenna with gain and the access point has a fixed antenna, this is a show stopper. The same is true with network connectivity, though there is more flexibility with network connections.

Fixed or Detachable Antenna

Because the antenna is an important part of the wireless infrastructure, an important part of the decision process is the selecting of an access point. It is never recommended that a fixed antenna be disconnected and a pigtail attached for remote antenna capability, mainly because this implementation requires that part of the inside of the access point be exposed to get the pigtail cable out of the access point case (which is not how it was intended to be installed).

If an external antenna is recommended by the site survey, it is important to make sure that an RP-TNC or SMA connector is part of the access point. The simple test is unscrewing the antenna from the access point; if this can be done, a remote antenna can be attached because the FCC mandates the type of connector that needs to be used for detachable antennas.

Wired Connectivity

In the past, making sure the access point had the correct connection capability to the wired network was a rule. Now it is an exception. Unless otherwise noted, all access points are purchased with a RJ45 connector for 10 Mbps 10BaseT Ethernet functionality. Beyond an RJ45 connector will depend on the vendor, and may include any number of the following connectors:

> ➤ 10/100BaseT
> ➤ 10Base2
> ➤ Fiber Optic
> ➤ Token Ring

Integration into Mobile Clients

There are different requirements for the many different types of mobile devices. In the past, developers of mobile clients have been concerned with the technology associated with the primary unit (processor, display, keyboard) as well as docking, batteries and battery chargers, etc. This means that not all devices that are radio capable are radio compatible, though today the industry is making large strides as many laptops have wireless radios integrated from the factory.

DESIGNED FOR RADIO?

This means that while there may be a technical capability to attach or integrate a radio for communication purposes, the device may be too noisy to be able to use internal radios (such as PC card, ISA bus, PCI bus) and may not have the connectivity (especially older workstations) to accommodate USB radios. It is important to understand all of the connectivity requirements that may be necessary for clients that will communicate on the wireless network.

PC CARD

The most common radio form factor has become the PCMCIA or PC card, because PC card slots are standard with most mobile devices (such as laptops, PDAs or industrial handheld mobile computers). The PC card provides connectivity from the device that it is inserted into the access points and other radios. Antennas on PC cards differ depending on the manufacturer of the card. It is important to understand the type of antenna and how it is mounted so that its performance can be integrated into your wireless solution. Most manufacturers use a patch antenna with the antenna facing up toward the front of the card and therefore upward when the card is inserted into a laptop.

COMPACT FLASH

Compact FLASH radio cards are similar to PC cards and are designed to be put inside of devices to provide wireless connectivity. Compact FLASH cards are very small and an excellent solution for PDAs and other devices with small footprints.

ISA AND PCI CARD

Wireless ISA or PCI cards are designed to be installed inside the desktop or server computer. These solutions today use PC cards to provide the radio functionality. The only caveat with these solutions is the recommendation that the same manufacturer is used for the radio that is used to provide the ISA or PCI card extension.

USB

USB clients are a fairly new addition to client connectivity, but are popular due to their ease of connectivity. Typically, USB clients are plug-and-play and get any necessary power from the client. The benefit of USB over ISA or PCI client adapters is that the implementation is external to the client, which means that the client device does not need to be opened up (which can void the warranty or introduce other issues). As with ISA and PCI client adapters, USB clients may be designed with internal PC cards. It is recommended that the radio not be interchanged with one from another manufacturer.

RS-232 AND ETHERNET CONVERTERS

Serial or Ethernet converters are the precursor to the USB client adapter. They are used with any device that has an Ethernet port or a 9 pin RS-232 port where it will be externally connected to the communication converter that connects the device to the wireless network.

Wireless Peripheral Enablement

Many times there is a need to connect a device to the wireless backbone that is not wireless enabled. This means that there is not a PC card or ISA capability to the device. Usually, this is a printer or scale that typically has a direct network connection and provides a service as a peripheral instead of processing information. Using the RS-232 port on these devices allows almost any device with a serial connection to utilize the wireless backbone to communicate. It is intended for use in networks that require the following:

  ➢   Stand alone scales
  ➢   Stand alone bar code printers
  ➢   Stand alone remote network printers
  ➢   Fixed stations that require a wireless connection
  ➢   Stand alone measurement equipment
  ➢   Programmable Logic Units (PLUs)

> Remote stand alone scanners
> Automatic Guided Vehicles (AGVs)
> Conveyor belts
> Industrial controllers
> Time and attendance
> Medical equipment

This connectivity flexibility allows users to create wireless solutions that maximize the wireless potential and not merely radio frequency data collection implementations that have a wireless infrastructure and mobile computers.

Questions and Useful Tips

❖ *Can I use a remote antenna with the PC card that I put into my laptop?*
> Technically, the answer is yes. This is not a general purpose solution, so it is important to understand what business problem this implementation is looking to resolve. The solution would require a pigtail to the SMA or TNC connector that is typically found on remote antennas.
❖ *Is there an advantage to having dumb access points connected to an intelligent network appliance?*
> The market has continually changed between distribution and centralization computing models.
❖ *Does wireless repeating rather than installing Ethernet to the access point reduce the cost of implementation?*
> This depends on whether the installation will be permanent. If it is, then does the cost of running the network cable exceed the additional access points that are necessary for wireless repeating? Value is provided by wireless repeating by being able to provide connection to network resources in areas where Ethernet cabling may not be able to be installed (or in temporary locations).
❖ *Some access points have the ability to support more than one radio. Is this important?*
> For most implementations this functionality does not add business value because the additional capability will not be used to meet the business problem. But yes, there are business problems where this functionality provides a more cost effective solution. For over ten years, vendors have offered the ability to support two radios in the same access point as a differentiator. There are several operational scenarios where two radios in the access point would be beneficial. The first scenario is where additional throughput is needed and a second

radio of the same frequency can be added without the additional cost of not only the access point but also the network cabling and power run to the access point. The second scenario involves the use of the second radio for building-to-building communications. In this case, the access point is placed on a wall where a patch antenna can be used to provide coverage inward into the facility and the antenna cable can be extended outside to a yagi or other point-to-point antenna for the other radio. In this second scenario, it also does not matter if the frequencies of the radios differ. For example, using 2.4 GHz internally and 5 GHz for the building-to-building connection is possible if this is best for the business problem that wireless communications is looking to solve. As a rule, two radios in an access point should not be a purchased option where the intent is using the second radio capability for upgrading, especially if the upgrade or additional radio is a different frequency. Because different frequencies have different coverage patterns and energy fall off rates, the positioning of the original access point may cause more access points to be purchased than if the second set was purchased separately.

❖ *My facility has a token ring or a token ring segment. Can I implement a wireless solution?*

➤ Yes, and there are several options that can be used. Some vendors have created token ring access points, though they tend to be much more expensive than their Ethernet counterparts. In order to use industry standard components and continue to ride the cost benefits of wireless that we have seen over time, it is recommended that a Token Ring to Ethernet translational bridge be used to create an Ethernet segment that can be used to install Ethernet access points. In the long run, this will be the most cost effective solution.

❖ *Can point-to-point bridges/routers use power over Ethernet?*

➤ Yes, some vendors support this option. It is important that this functionality be verified before the purchase of the equipment if it is required.

❖ *Can I monitor the performance on point-to-point and point to multipoint bridges/routers?*

➤ Yes, most companies have tools that will allow network managements to see the traffic that is being sent over the wireless link.

Implementation System Issues Affecting Wireless LANs

Overview

A wireless LAN solution is more than just the radios or the access point and mobile clients that contain the radio. Wireless communications are a transport that is an extension of the wired LAN. Because it supports many of the same applications as the enterprise wired network, it needs to be governed by the same principles and policies as its wired counterpart. This means that if the wired network has been designed to be fault tolerant or fault resilient, this needs to be addressed with the wireless network. Other specific issues may also include areas where there is a need for additional performance or where power cannot be routed.

The same cohesiveness and consistency between the wired and wireless transports goes for other enterprise issues such as security, device management and network management. It is important to realize that an "extension of the wired LAN" means more than just the physical layer transport.

Throughput

One of the basic questions associated with wireless LANs is "How much throughput will it have?" The final answer to the question depends on many factors, including whether the question was directed toward a single access point or the entire wireless infrastructure, the size of messages that are using the wireless infrastructure and the number of people trying to send a message at any one particular moment in time. In the past, wireless vendors had to try to squeeze data throughput out of smaller data pipes such as 4.8 or 9.6 Kbps and as a result the CDMA transmission protocol is more efficient that wired protocols. In respect to raw throughput of a wireless LAN the rule of thumb is that the CDMA protocol allows approximately 50% of the data rate to be used for data throughput. This means that, in general, an 11 Mbps wireless LAN will provide 5 Mbps throughput for application. Similarly an Ethernet network using CSMA which will have more collisions and retries will have a 30% throughput compared to the quoted data rate.

If you are not getting the throughput that is expected, check the size of the message setting on the access point for the radio. Some access point manufacturers' default settings are for the maximum wireless packet, which is larger than the maximum Ethernet packet. This means that if the application is sending a large amount of data, packets are forced to be fragmented at the access point so that it can be put on the Ethernet, which may impact throughput.

Transaction Density

Transaction density, in combination with peak transactions, have been the most common misunderstanding encountered by customers when installing wireless networks. Transaction density is the amount of data that can be transmitted and received by a single access point during a period of time.

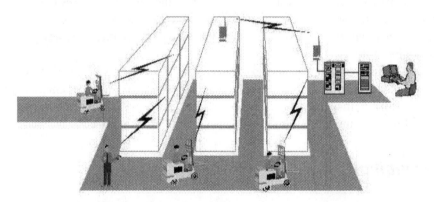

The problem can be explained through the following example. Assume that a facility, either an office or a warehouse, has twenty installed access points. Yet while the entire facility has wireless coverage, 50% of the users or more are associated with or connected to a single access point. Essentially, these 50% are using a single point of access to the network; response time may be slow when everyone is waiting to communicate. In a warehouse scenario, this typically applies to an area where everyone checks out his or her data collection device, turns it on and logs in. With anywhere from 20 to 100 users standing in a single location, everyone wonders why response time is slow. As everyone spreads out and continues to work (accessing the wireless network at different times using different access points), the response time appears to speed up and provide instantaneous service.

Peak Transactions

While transaction density applies to a spike that is limited geographically (such as a single coverage area), "peak transactions" are defined as high transactions over the entire wireless network, but over time. The number and size of the transactions is a good measure of how the network, both wired and wireless, needs to be sized. While users tend to provide information about their usage and number of transactions over an extended period of time (such as 24 hours), usage must be measured in smaller time increments, such as minutes or, ultimately, seconds.

In the past, customers measured the number of transactions in a 24-hour period during which they were manually inputting the data into the system. Without understanding the peak transaction rate, vendors often assume that the use of the wireless network is uniform or that the transactions are spread out evenly over the time period. Unfortunately, this is rarely true; often, 80% of the usage is completed in 20% of the time. Without understanding the peak transaction rate, the performance at the customer site may be perceived as slow.

Increasing Performance

One of the ways to address transaction density is to increase the performance in the area where there is high density. This can be accomplished by adding additional access points to a single coverage area. With UHF, the process of increasing the available wireless bandwidth requires getting another frequency allocated to the geographical location, which takes time and expense. Additionally, the mobile clients need to be allocated to a specific access point. As technology has improved, synthesized UHF radios are able to be aware of multiple available legal frequencies and move between them. For spread spectrum technologies, multiple access points can be added to increase the performance of the coverage area. This can also be referred to as "stacking" access points, as the logical coverage areas are layered one on top of the other.

"Stacking" Access Points

If multiple access points are stacked in a single coverage area, it is important that the channels be coordinated to prevent as much interference as possible.

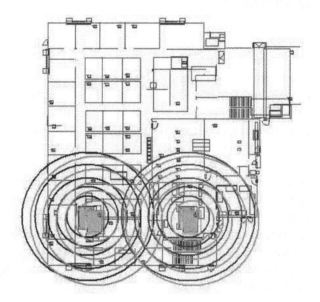

In proprietary vendor specific solutions (such as 900 MHz and non-standard 2.4 GHz solutions), the ability to stack access points to improve performance may or may not be a function of the system. If non-standards based solution is being used or considered, it is important to check or ask about this functionality. As an example, in one proprietary implementation, the 900 MHz radio used the entire radio frequency spectrum and there was no capability to stack access points. This tradeoff was used because the design emphasis was on interference robustness and fault resilience because a "hot" backup could be installed to continually "listen" as a secondary access point, and become active only if the "primary" access point failed.

Load Balancing

Load balancing is a feature where in the event that clients have multiple choices of access points to connect, the client would connect to the one that had the lowest utilization. Multiple-choice scenarios can occur when access point coverage is overlapped, when redundancy is important, or stacked, when performance is the high priority. While the primitives for load balancing are part of the IEEE 802.11 a,b and g specifications, load balancing is not a feature of the standard. Because it is not part of the standard, load balancing is a feature that is vendor specific and may require getting the access points from a single vendor if this is an important feature. If load balancing is important, then the next question pertains to the algorithm that is used by the vendor to implement load balancing. The three basic algorithms are number of clients attached to the access point, bandwidth utilization, and signal strength. Each implementation has its pluses and minuses. For example, an implementation that uses the number of clients could be a problem if your client attaches to access point that has only one other client but it is downloading large files and has high bandwidth utilization. Likewise, the access point with the highest signal strength may have a large number of clients attached and while bandwidth utilization is a good measure of the capability to communicate with minimum signal strength the client may spend a lot of time reattaching because it continues to lose the signal. Most successful implementations will use a combination of these algorithm components plus perhaps others, but the vendor should be able to explain the rational for the algorithm implementation, and it should apply to the business problem that is being solved.

SPATIAL REUSE

Spatial reuse occurs in any CDMA solution where there is disjoint coverage. Basically if two access points cannot hear each other because of their distance, they can transmit or receive at the same time. This functionality allows the throughput of the wireless network to increase by the number of access points that have disjoint coverage.

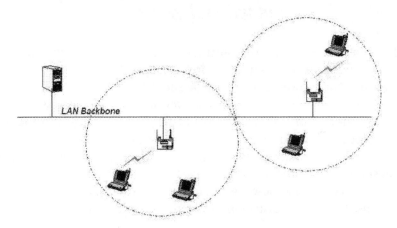

Locking in the Performance in the Coverage Cell

The IEEE 802.11 standard allows for automatic fallback of the data rate. This means that further away from the access point the client travels the weaker the signal and ability to maintain a higher data rate. For IEEE 802.11b the supported data rates in the specification are 11, 5.5, 2 and 1 Mbps. For some applications especially with known high throughput requirements, it is important to make sure that the entire coverage area is capable of high throughput, for IEEE 802.11 that would be 11 Mbps and for 802.11g it would be 54 Mbps. In these cases, the site survey can be done to assure that highest data rate is maintained. The problem is that depending on the roaming algorithm that is used by the client it may stay attached to an access point as it moves away and out of the high throughput coverage dropping automatically to the lower throughput fallback speeds. For this reason, it is important to make sure that the vendor has the capability of turning off the fall back capability of the access point and therefore forcing the roam to another high speed access point. It is important to understand if all access points that are being deployed have this capability in the set up. There is nothing to preclude that the site survey could not have been completed with a 54 Mbps requirement using IEEE 802.11g for 2.4 GHz communications. The only issue with "locking" in the throughput is that all clients that attach to the network must have the capability of supporting the throughput. For example, if the wireless communication network was locked in at 54 Mbps without fallback capability, IEEE 802.11b radios operating at 11 Mbps would not be able to use the network.

Extending Coverage without Wires

When operations expand or construction causes the restructuring of the facility, it may become necessary to address changes that have occurred in the coverage area. These coverage holes can be addressed through several methodologies the simplest is to redo the site survey and move the access points to provide the maximum coverage. Unfortunately this option is also the most expensive because it includes possibly moving power and Ethernet cabling to the location of the new access points. Another potential solution, and the one used most often, is to identify the coverage holes and install new access points to provide the coverage. If power is already available at the location, there is an option to use the wireless distribution system or wireless hopping.

WIRELESS HOPPING

Wireless hopping uses two radios to provide communication for the coverage area where one of the radios is serving as the Ethernet connection to the backbone infrastructure and other radio is providing the coverage for the clients. This functionality is not used often because the cost of access points has dropped and most implementers have found it easier and more reliable to install the power and network cabling to the needed area.

MESHING

Meshing is the ability to send a message with an unknown path. A client using meshing may send a message that is transmitted to another client who sends it to an access point because the first client could not hear the access point. The path may have many intermediary transmission points before it reaches it destination or a wired infrastructure. This functionality works well if the wireless client is not mobile, such as a wireless office environment. But in many applications where the clients move through the facility, the ability to communicate is impaired if a client does not have direct access to an access point.

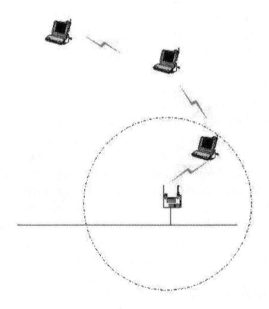

Interference

If the installation uses UHF radio frequencies, the FCC provides protection from interference sources that may prevent communication on the channel that has been allocated. Addressing interference in the spread spectrum frequencies is much different; especially as all radio sources are expected to be able to use the spectrum independently. Interference may present itself in a number of ways, including narrowband interference, interference across the entire band, signal degradation or side band interference that may occur from a radio using an adjacent channel. Additionally, the interference is not necessarily from other radios or wireless LANs; interference in the selected frequency may be due to the manufacturing process or occur naturally.

NARROWBAND INTERFERENCE

Narrowband interference is a signal that is typically a narrow frequency (as the name suggests), has high output power relative to other signals and may be constant or intermittent. Because it is "narrowband" interference, it does not interfere with all of the channels in the spectrum. It interferes only with the one where it occurs and, depending on the power output, the adjacent channels. This means that if interference occurs in channel 5, the communications on channel 1 or channel 11 are not affected. For example, some RF ID tags operating in 900 MHz spectrum sit in the middle of the spectrum at 915 MHz and have been used by automakers to track products (such as engine blocks or cars) through the manufacturing process. The high power signal, when used for this automation process, spreads beyond the 915 MHz signal. This makes the middle part of the band useable and allows only the beginning and end of the 900 MHz band to be used by other applications. Other applications in the 900 MHz band include spread spectrum phones or garage door openers, which use a narrow band signal close to the beginning of the band.

In order to detect this narrowband interference, some wireless LAN vendors include a software spectrum analyzer as part of the site survey tool. This product can be loaded on a desktop or laptop that has a radio installed and can be used to detect potential interference. Most site survey results will look for, describe and recommend avoidance for interference.

ACROSS BAND INTERFERENCE

Whereas narrowband interference occurs in a few narrowly located frequencies, across band interference occurs across the entire frequency range. In the 2.4 GHz spectrum, this may occur in operations where microwaves are used for welding plastic as part of the manufacturing process. This is why one of the first troubleshooting questions asked concerning 2.4 GHz wireless interference is whether the facility has microwaves. This not only includes microwaves used for business practices but also the microwaves in the break room or cafeteria. Microwave ovens can leak one watt or more into the spectrum without any notice, especially older, high power microwaves. The power is many times stronger than the signal received by an access point. Other issues include the fact that microwave power output typically runs on a 50% duty cycle, which makes it intermittent. If the offending microwave is in the break room it may be used only during certain times of the day. Besides microwaves, interference may occur as part of the product testing process, such as a spark plug manufacturer where interference is present across not only the radio spectrums but also others.

ADJACENT CHANNEL INTERFERENCE

Adjacent channels are those channels that are side by side. In the IEEE 802.11 standard, they significantly overlap each other because the channels are 22 MHz wide, but the center frequencies for each channel are only 5 MHz apart. Adjacent channel interference occurs when two or more access points have channels that overlap to the point of interference. This issue should be addressed by the site survey, which will indicate which channels should be used by each recommended access point. It is especially important to check adjacent channel interference potential if an additional access point is being installed to increase performance in a given area.

Power Over Ethernet

Power over Ethernet (PoE) is a method of delivering DC power to an access point over the Ethernet cable for the purpose of powering the unit. PoE is used when AC power is not available. Power over Ethernet access points are available only for 2.4 GHz or higher. They are viable because the coverage area in most installations does not exceed the maximum Ethernet cat5 single cable run length of 100 yards (100 meters). The cost of a PoE implementation needs to be weighed against the installation costs of power to the access points. Additionally, there are several issues (such as the lack of an industry standard on the implementation of PoE and varying necessary input voltages for different vendor access points) that point to a recommendation that the entire PoE solution be purchased from a single vendor.

Non-Ethernet Wired Infrastructures

While Ethernet is the majority of wired infrastructures installed, other wired solutions, such as token ring and fiber optic, continue to exist. Technologies such as token ring existed before the introduction of wireless, whereas fiber was being introduced to the market at the same time as wireless. *When* the technology became available for IT departments to deploy played heavily on how wireless was integrated with the physical wired backbone.

TOKEN RING

When wireless was first introduced in vertical market data collection solutions, token ring was already prevalent in the industrial marketplace and being used for mission critical applications. Ethernet was just getting its feet wet in the early 1990's, and at the time, token ring was a much more stable technology. In order to address market needs, companies such as Proxim and Teklogix introduced access points that could be directly connected to token ring. While the vendor companies addressed issues such as source route bridging, wireless over token ring had limited success. Many companies with existing token ring are opting for translational bridges to convert the physical layer from token ring to Ethernet and then using Ethernet technology, including access points, to deploy wireless coverage.

Wireless Fault Tolerance and Fault Resilience

In many vertical market applications, the wireless infrastructure is part of a mission critical application. Access point failures or coverage holes where the application could not function could mean hundreds of thousands of dollars in stopped operations or lost productivity. For this reason, systems integrators began to design solutions that were fault resilient or had no single point of failure.

OVERLAPPING COVERAGE

All of the discussion on the radio signal has been limited to single access point solutions. It is important to remember that a portion of coverage is also used to provide overlapping coverage so that wireless clients can seamlessly roam from one cell to another. Overlapping coverage is also used to provide seamless coverage in the event of an access point failure. Two adjacent access points provided redundant coverage while providing an additional benefit of additional throughput at the same time.

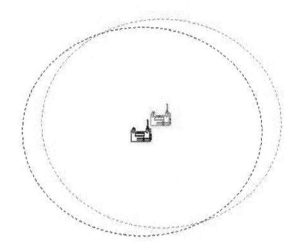

WIRELESS ACCESS POINT

If the solution includes wireless access points for redundancy, then the coverage will be significantly less than single access points or simple overlapping coverage scenarios. This is because a wireless access point must be able to transmit and receive from adjacent access points. This scenario is used in sites that have requested fault tolerant wireless solutions.

Network Addresses—Using DHCP

For any wireless network, keeping track of the addresses can be a hassle (whether it is a proprietary numeric based address scheme or IP based). This hassle can only be multiplied if we are trying to synchronize the addresses on multiple subnets (whether the clients are mobile or not). Fortunately, the network community recognized this problem and there are multiple painless solutions to the situation, depending on the environment. Dynamic Host Communication Protocol (DHCP) allows clients using TCP/IP to automatically get an IP address. This is recommended for all mobile clients.

In an independent wireless system, such as a tool crib application or a temporary location that is not attached to the enterprise network, there is not an IP network and the company has not been assigned a set of IP addresses. Here, DCHP can be used with a 10 net address (RFC 1918) or private address space for the segment. The 10 net addressing is intended for internal use only and consists of 10.0.0.0 addresses, which can be used by most access points that have DHCP server functionality integrated into the access point. If the network is to be attached to an enterprise network, the 10 net IP address should be changed to meet the assigned IP address structure for the company.

If the solution is part of a larger enterprise, a DCHP server may already be part of the solution. If so, this server can be used to assign IP addresses to mobile clients. It is important to have a single DHCP server to source IP addressing information. If the enterprise centralizes address assignment with DHCP, it is important to take advantage of the established, reliable DHCP service by using DHCP relay; the individual subnet request is relayed back to the centralized server.

SPECIAL ATTENTION FOR ACCESS POINTS

For troubleshooting purposes, it is important to know the address of the access points. In a DHCP environment, a power glitch may or parameter change may cause the access point to reset. In a DHCP environment, there is no guarantee that the IP address previously assigned will be the new IP address. This same scenario occurs when the lease expires on the address that has been assigned to the access point. Now the network administrator is in the dark about where the access point is located.

It is recommended for access points that the IP address be static so that the network administrator will always know what the IP address is for a given access point. This recommendation also allows the IP address to be posted with the access point to be used as an identifier if there is any user identified problem, such as a broken antenna or dead spot. This may also be used in conjunction with Domain Name Services (DNS) to give an alphabetic name to the access point. If a static IP address cannot be given to the access point, then minimally assure that the access point has an infinite lease for the IP address that it gets when it powers up. This means that the lease will not expire and that the AP will continually get new addresses.

DHCP and Security

It is important to verify as part of system testing that there are no issues or undesirable interaction between address assignment and security. If a VPN is deployed for security, it may be necessary to use RFC 1918 (private) address space for the infrastructure until the VPN authentication succeeds.

Wireless Security

Overview

While anytime and anywhere communications continue to be important to business success, protecting corporate information users from outside "forces of evil" has become a new priority. Wireless security has become an important issue to network administrators who want to keep the bad guys at bay while providing the needed flexibility to users. Security continues to be the most significant but least understood and appreciated element of communications and information technology. Due to a lack of understanding of the risks, the majority of wireless networks are running without adequate security measures or policies. Because wireless LANs are inherently less secure than their wired counterparts this creates security vulnerabilities that if not addressed allow the door to opened to hackers. A good security solution needs to stress simplicity and ease of operation while not compromising the security or its effectiveness. An FBI study shows that 72% of all Fortune 100 companies have experienced a security breach of some type, and network administrators continue to strive to shut the door to potential attacks. A research company in the UK reported that 67% of companies with wireless LANs employed no encryption at all and the remaining 33% used only the IEEE 802.11 provided WEP. The Gartner Group reports that without security beyond the current IEEE 802.11 WEP implementation, 30% of enterprises will suffer serious security exposures from deploying wireless LANs. Understanding and implementing wireless security measures is not a "learn as you go" endeavor. In order to sort out the hazards that are presented by implementing a wireless LAN, it is important first understand the issues associated with wireless security, which security measures are needed and why and then how to apply the lessons learned to secure the assets that need to be protected. Whether a wireless LAN is part of the enterprise infrastructure communication strategy or not, it is important that every company have a wireless security policy, even if it is to say that wireless LANs are not allowed to access the enterprise infrastructure. Like most communication infrastructures, if a wireless LAN exists, there is the possibility of someone try-ing to "intrude" sometimes unintentionally but sometimes intentionally.

UNDERSTANDING THE SECURITY RISK

Intentional intrusion can be simply defined as knowingly being someplace that you shouldn't be. Typically it consists of someone using network resources such as access to the internet that they are not authorized to access, pretending to be someone that they are not in order to use resources/data or causing the media to be non-functional and not allowing anyone to have access to the resources or data. While these same issues present themselves on any media, wired or wireless, IT administrator now have the tools to be able to design and implement wired security policies that will deter an intruder. With the perva-sive use of wireless technology, the industry is now applying the appropriate "lessons learned" to wireless solutions.

Unauthorized Access

Unauthorized access is the most common of wireless security breaches because it occurs where an individual or company is not deploying any secu-rity methodology. Once the intruder enters the open door of a non-secured wireless network, the resulting actions fall into two categories depending on the intent of the intruder; either a casual snooper or a criminal hacker. If an intruder is accessing the network to gain access to the internet and their intent is typically not to harm the individual or company, they fall into the casual snooper. While this may be a victimless crime, it is comparable to the person who splices into his neighbors cable line so that he does not have to pay for it. It is easy to imagine this type of unauthorized access in an apartment complex, a retail strip mall or a multi-story building.

Whereas if an intruder accesses the network or hijacks the identity of a per-son with the intent to gain and use or change the data that that person has access to, the intruder is much more dangerous and falls into the criminal hacker category. Imagine the same apartment complex where now the access is to the home computer that also does PC banking and has passwords stored on it. Looking at the same strip mall retail store or multi-story office building, the wireless network may also allow access to the ISP, in store processor, where credit card information is stored or office server with personnel information. Even though the POS, point of sale, registers or the human resource computers are wired, the wireless network may allow access to the same server and data-base where critical information is stored. Additionally, consider the inverse to getting data "from the network," once the intruder is connected consider data insertion. In this scenario, the intruder loads a trojan program or virus onto a server or loads confidential competitive information or pornography onto the server. Again data insertion can occur in either the home computer or company scenarios whether it is an apartment, strip mall or corporate facility.

Wireless LAN Discovery

Wireless standards have brought wireless LAN communications to the mainstream and as companies realize the benefits of wireless, they also need to be aware of the hazards. One of the biggest security problems of IT administrators as well as residential users is to use the factory defaults that are supplied by the manufacturer and even with the known risks over 25% of wireless access points are still using the defaults. Changing the defaults does not make the LAN safe because there are discovery tools that will provide the information, such as NetStumbler. NetStumbler is a free Windows based wireless utility that can be loaded on a laptop and used with several different PC card radios that allow external antennas to be attached to the wireless LAN card in order to find wireless networks in the coverage area of the radio card. If a person has a laptop in their car with a wireless card attached to a directional (focused beam, increased distance) or omnidirectional (circular coverage, less distance) antenna, they can drive around business parks or residential areas looking for wireless networks. NetStumbler operates by scanning for IEEE 802.11b wireless networks in either infrastructure or point to point mode and provides the following information about the wireless network:

- MAC address
- SSID
- Access Point name
- Channel
- Radio manufacturer
- Whether WEP is turned on or off
- Signal Strength

The first point of access is finding out the SSID of the access point and if WEP is turned off, as it is with most factory default settings, an intruder can attach to the network by setting the SSID of his or her wireless card to the wireless network. The intruder can now attach to the network has access to all of the resources on the network as if they were any other computer on the network. This is an especially important note for residential users because this also gives the intruder access to shared hard drives which may contain personal or financial information when they log in as a guest to any computer depending on the operating system or network configuration.

At a corporate level, once attached to the network, standard network management tools can use SNMP to discover additional nodes on the network. This is important because this allows discovery and potentially access to the enterprise network through a remote or branch office that is connected via the WAN to the corporate infrastructure.

Unauthorized Clients

It should not surprise anyone that there are people who drive around and look for open wireless networks, and there is currently a website that actually documents and updates these networks. It is no wonder that a security policy is very important, especially one that incorporates wireless. Whether it is someone in the next house, next apartment, store next door in a retail mall, floor above or below in an office building or in a car outside in the parking lot, unauthorized clients require only a laptop, a radio (which today is often already integrated into the laptop or can be purchased separately for less than $100) and appropriate software off the internet. It should also be noted that this does not apply only to IEEE 802.11 (a,b or g) infrastructures but can also be problem for older 2.4 GHz or 900 MHz solutions. While these solutions are proprietary in nature, OpenAir, Spectrum24, Aironet or other implementations may be more vulnerable because they have limited security countermeasures (such as a pseudo SSID) that are often broadcast in the clear where the intruder is attached. Industrial and retail companies that still have these solutions often note the issues with obtaining these radios, the difficulty in connecting the radio (most are not PC card) and the increased expense associated with their purchase. While all of these points are true and they may deter a hacker looking for an easy mark, it is important to note that the security hole still exists and that if it is exploited the only current viable countermeasure is 100% replacement of the infrastructure and devices because there are no hardware or firmware upgrade paths and many client devices are incapable of running a VPN or other higher layer countermeasures.

Rogue Access Points

Unauthorized clients are not the only way to attach to the network; sometimes an access point is used. When any access point is attached (either wired or wirelessly) to a personal or corporate network without authorization, it is called a "rogue" access point. While rogue access points are often thought of as being used by the criminal hacker, this scenario may also be in a company without any wireless network with an employee looking for a productivity tool to help with his or her job. In either case, the access point is unauthorized and has opened a door to the network that others may also use to access the network.

In order to counter rogue access point, IT managers must look to detect them, and that means being proactive. One of the most common methods of being proactive is to sniff the network to see if any wireless, or the right wireless, is being used. To no surprise, the same tools that are used in wireless LAN discovery (such as NetStumbler) by intruders are now being used by IT managers to audit or discover devices that should or should not be part of the network infrastructure. If more than an occasional audit is needed, the wireless community has probes that sit on the network and constantly monitor the wireless "ether" for unauthorized traffic.

Denial of Service

While network packet analyzers allow the intruder to decode and view intercepted traffic, sometimes that is not the intent of the intruder. Once connected to the LAN, the intruder may begin to flood the link with traffic, making it difficult to use the wireless network (and depending on the backbone, may cause problems with other applications due to the latency injected onto the network). This version of a denial of service attack can cause significant operational problems for unsecure wireless networks.

EXISTING SECURITY ISSUES WITH IEEE 802.11 AND 802.11B

Security for a wireless LAN is the process of ensuring that only trusted users gain access to network resources. The basic problem with the current IEEE 802.11 implementation is that it provides security based on the computer, not the user. Plus, it does not provide authentication of the user once he or she is authorized to use the network resources. The security aspect of IEEE 802.11 currently has four components: Service Set Identification (SSID), Association Negotiation, MAC Address Authentication and Wired Equivalent Privacy (WEP). Unfortunately, all of these components are flawed individually, as well as combined, from a security standpoint. Typically, all of the information needed to access the network is contained on a laptop or personal computer that can be stolen or lost. Additionally, no password is needed to access the network.

Service Set Identifier (SSID)

While the SSID can be used to keep the casual or accidental intruder off of the wireless network, by itself the SSID is broadcast in the open per the 802.11 standard and is available to anyone who is listening with a sniffer. A sniffer is a software package that looks at network packets; it can be connected to a wired LAN or with a radio card to a wireless LAN. The SSID is like an SNMP (Simple Network Management Protocol) community string or VLAN ID; it defines an administrative domain but is not a security mechanism.

Some access points provide support to turn off the access point (AP) broadcast of the SSID; however, a wireless client trying to associate (connect) to an AP which they will when the attempt to roam, the AP will send the SSID in the clear, again per the IEEE 802.11 standard, and when the AP accepts the association a hacker will know that the SSID is valid.

802.11 Association Negotiation

There are two methods of association negotiation that can be used: shared key and open authentication. This negotiation is used by access points to allow wireless clients to connect.

Shared Key

Shared key authentication involves sending a challenge and then receiving an encrypted version of the challenge. Shared key authentication has a fatal flaw because both the challenge and the encrypted challenge are available to be sniffed by a hacker. This means that a hacker could use the challenge and the response to authenticate using the same initialization vector (IV). It is not recommended that shared key authentication be used for associating to an access point.

Open Authentication

Open authentication involves sending a challenge, but the AP declares the authentication successful without sending the return encrypted message.

MAC Address Authentication

MAC address authentication involves a "training" period that creates a table of MAC addresses that will be allowed to associate to an AP. One of the problems is that the MAC address is contained in every packet that is sent. Again, it is a trivial effort to sniff a network and determine one or more valid MAC addresses, and unfortunately it is not much harder to spoof a MAC address onto the network. Additionally, radio cards can be lost or stolen, and without retraining the access points they would still be valid on the wireless network. MAC authentication can be a administration headache for an IT manager when new equipment needs to be added to the authentication table, especially when it comes to service units which may go in and out of service.

Wired Equivalent Privacy (WEP)

WEP is the basic security method provided by the IEEE 802.11 standard and was designed to provide security equivalent to a wired network using a shared key of either 40 or 104 bits. Most people think that encryption is 64 or 128 bit key, but the first 24 bits contain the initialization vector (IV). And while the client changes the IV with every packet, it is included in each packet sent in the clear. The combination of the IV+WEB key gives the size of 64 bit or 128 bit. The packet also includes an integrity check value (ICV). WEP provides basic encryption but not effective authentication.

To get a packet, the WEP key and IV are combined and run through a cipher, such as RC4, to generate a varying key stream. The stream and the message text to be encrypted are XORed to create the text that is sent in the packet. Rivest Cipher #4 or RC4 is licensed from RSA and is the same algorithm built into standard web browsers (Secure Socket Layer or SSL).

WEP Vulnerabilities

There are several vulnerabilities that are part of the IEEE 802.11 WEP implementation that need to be addressed in any wireless security policy. WEP by itself is not enough, for the following reasons:

➤ 40 bit WEP key is too small.

   Brute force attacks on a 40 bit key can take anywhere from fifteen minutes to several days. A similar attack on the 104-bit key takes billions of years. Security analysts note that 128 bit WEP is pretty secure—but only if the key is changed (which addresses other WEP issues).

➤ Weak Initialization Vector

   A weak initialization vector can lead to passive discovery of the WEP key. Products such as AirSnort and wepcrack can exploit this weakness.

➤ Initialization Vector Replay

   When selecting the initialization vector, traditional logic does not prevail. A random selection of IVs will lead to reuse in an average of 5,000 packets. It is recommended that IVs be used sequentially, and that when the end of the list is reached the starting point be selected randomly.

➢ Known Packet Attack

In TCP/IP, responses to messages are known whether they are encrypted or not. Additionally, many packets start with the same sequence (such as TCP/IP) where the addresses are in the beginning of the packet. Sending a known packet to a wireless client will result in revealing the key stream.

➢ Bit Flipping

Bit flipping allows bits to be flipped to change the IP address to the hackers address and fix the ICV as well as the IP sum and retransmit on wireless. The AP sees a valid packet, decrypts it and sends it to the hacker decrypted.

EXISTING LEGACY WLANS

The market currently contains previous generation UHF, 900 MHz and non-standards based 2.4 GHz wireless network solutions. These solutions are also called legacy wireless LANs. While they have not been available in form factors that can be integrate into laptops for rogue activities they can still be connected. Because most legacy solutions have only pseudo SSIDs which were incorporated to provide separation of other LANs in close proximity, once connect a sniffer can be used to monitor traffic to decode packets or insert a denial of service attack. Another is that legacy wireless solutions require being locked into a single vendor, a higher cost implementation and limited availability.

ENCRYPTION AND AUTHENTICATION

The two primary needs of securing wireless networks are encryption and authentication. Encryption is a means of disguising or scrambling messages which makes them unreadable by anyone who does not have the "secret" or key. Authentication is means of authorization that makes sure that the gives wireless clients access to the network by making sure that are who they say they are before they are attached to the network.

ADDRESSING CUSTOMER ENCRYPTION NEEDS

Given time and resources, almost any encryption scheme can be broken. One of the secrets for successful encryption algorithms is to change the key before it is known. The WEP solution provided in IEEE 802.11 does not provide a secure mechanism for transmitting packets.

IEEE 802.11i

IEEE 802.11i introduces the following changes to provide additional encryption. It is important to note that 802.11i, while correcting issues with encryption, does not provide authentication. While 802.11i also provide encryption of management frames the major features of this solution are temporal key integrity protocol (TKIP) and the advanced encryption services (AES) which strengthen the protection of data on wireless networks.

Temporal Key Integrity Protocol (TKIP)

TKIP uses WEP and increases the size of the key from 40 to 128 bits, but instead of using a WEP key to encrypt all packets, TKIP encrypts each packet into one of 500 trillion possible combinations. TKIP works within the 802.1x framework and has four basic functions: creating the temporal key from the master key, distribution of the temporal keys to the system, mixing the key to provide an RC4 per packet key and providing the message integrity check (MIC) to prevent replay attacks.

The implementation of MIC adds 16 additional bytes to the message but prevents an attacker from capturing data packets, changing them and then resending them on the network.

Advanced Encryption Services (AES)

AES replaces RC4 in the WEP scheme and provides better encryption. It has already been adopted as an official government standard by the US Department of Commerce and the National Institute of Standards and Technology (NIST). While AES is capable of employing variable key sizes of 128, 192 or 256 bit kits, the biggest pushback in respect to AES is that it will require hardware changes in currently deployed wireless radios in order to implement the encryption scheme.

Encryption of Management Frames

Encryption of the management frames also prevents additional information that may be gleaned to get information about the network.

ADDRESSING CUSTOMER AUTHENTICATION NEEDS

Authentication is a fairly new requirement to the wireless arena, though it has always been part of wired security solutions. For wireless solutions, the customer is looking for an authentication method that encompasses the following:

- ➤ Authenticates in both directions. This makes it more difficult to bring up rogue access points and makes man in the middle attacks more challenging.
- ➤ Can be used to drive WEP keys.
- ➤ Is not vulnerable to dictionary attacks
- ➤ Is relatively fast and efficient, so that a large processor and extended battery power is required to implement.
- ➤ Provides a high level of security.
- ➤ Is not too costly to administrate.

IEEE 802.1x

IEEE 802.1x offers an effective framework for authenticating and controlling user traffic to a protected network. 802.1x ties a protocol called EAP (Extensible Authentication Protocol) to both the wired and wireless LAN media and supports multiple authentication methods.

With the new framework comes new terms, specifically supplicant, authenticator and authentication server. A *supplicant* is a component that requests access to the network. This communication is done through a protocol called EAL-OL. The *authenticator* is an access point in the wireless community. The authenticator passes the information to an *authentication server*. This communication protocol is called EAP-RADIUS. The server verifies if the user has access to the network through one of the authentication methods discussed below.

MD5

MD5 was the earliest EAP authentication type. This essentially duplicates CHAP password protection on a WLAN. MD5 represents a kind of base-level EAP support among 802.1x devices. MD5 is not recommended as an authentication protocol because it does not facilitate the generation of keys and is easy to break. The only thing that MD5 is recommended for is as a test tool in the lab to make sure that the RADIUS server is running correctly.

Lightweight EAP (LEAP)

LEAP is a proprietary authentication that has been developed by Cisco. While it provides moderate authentication, it is known for its wide operating system support and recommended only to be used when TLS or TTLS are not available (such as with UNIX or MAC operating systems). LEAP uses username/password authentication and therefore is subject to dictionary attacks if the passwords aren't strong. In addition to sending the username in the clear, roaming from one access point to another can take up to 3 seconds and therefore is a problem for mobile environments.

Transport Layer Security (TLS)

TLS is a certificate-based authentication method that requires both the supplicant (client device) and the authenticator (server) to have valid certificates. If the customer already uses certificates, this is a good choice as certifications are an extra expense.

Tunneled TLS (TTLS)

Tunneled TLS uses TLS to authenticate the server side with a certificate and to establish an encrypted tunnel. Once the tunnel is encrypted, there are a plethora of methods that can be used for authentication, including the following:

➤ Clear text passwords. This allows a proxy server to authenticate to legacy applications.
➤ Challenge-response passwords.
➤ One-time passwords.
➤ Certificates.

The key to a TTLS implementation is that the encrypted tunnel can set up anonymously, so there is no information in sniffed packets.

Protected EAP (PEAP)

PEAP is the Microsoft initiative that is very similar to TTLS. PEAP stresses the use of any EAP authentication method, such as MD5 or certificates, once the tunnel is established whereas TTLS allows any authentication method.

Secure Remote Password (SRP)

SRP provides good authentication but has several commercial issues. Namely, it is computationally intensive (which can cause a problem for mobile devices that are looking to use their process for the application instead of computing packet information). Additionally, Stanford University has filed IP concerning SRP, and a licensing arrangement is needed to implement it.

Wi-Fi Protected Access (WPA)

WPA is a specification that has been created by the Wi-Fi alliance, a group of wireless industry product manufacturers, to address the security needs from the identification of the weakness in WEP in the original IEEE 802.11 standard to the ratification of IEEE 802.11i, which provide resolution to the issues. The WPA specification addresses both encryption and authentication. A WPA implementation increases the WEP keys to 128 and provides automatically distribution of dynamic keys which are session based. It is essentially the IEEE 802.11i TKIP implementation without AES. As for authentication, WPA uses IEEE 802.1x to provide strong user authentication.

Higher Layer Security Methods

Security can also be addressed above the physical layer using traditional wired technology solutions such as virtual private networking (VPNs) or virtual local area networks (VLANs) at the network layer, layer 3 in the OSI reference architecture.

Virtual Private Networks

Customers that have already implemented end-to-end VPNs for their wired clients because the outside users are going through a firewall for some of the applications are extending them to include wireless applications. Because these customers already have ports to support VPN, either unused ports can be used for additional ports added to the solution to use the VPN for their wireless applications inside of the firewall. The primary issue is the cost initially associated with implementing a VPN, and therefore, this typically applies to a customer site that already has the solution deployed in the site.

There are several benefits of VPNs, including seamless roaming as well as no WEP keys or MAC addresses to administer. The biggest issues with VPN as the only solution is that VPNs are layer three security solutions, which mean that hackers can attack the network before log on and before log off. Additionally, VPNs provide protection for the data on the network but not the network itself, which would allow a hacker to use other network resources.

Virtual Local Area Networks (VLANs)

Virtual local area networks created in switched environments allow users only to access the subnet that is defined by the VLAN. While this solution allows access only to a restricted subnet, it does not prevent access onto the physical network. Again, the data is protected but the network is not, and is analogous to tapping into an Ethernet port of the same segment (but have access only to the subnet resource).

WIRELESS LAN SECURITY BEST PRACTICES

The following recommendations should be implemented for a secure corporate wireless network:

> **Have a wireless security policy.** The company's security policy should include wireless network. This should include configuration, installation and placement recommendations in the network topology as well as authorization and authentication mechanisms.

> **Reduce the amount of radio signal outside the building.** The coverage area of the wireless infrastructure can be controlled by the internal antenna design that is part of the site survey, which is highly recommended for corporate users. Make sure that the company that does the site survey is aware that there should not be any extraneous coverage outside the facility unless otherwise noted. Additionally if anything has changed in the structure such as moving a wall or the contents in the building, then it is important to measure the coverage which may have been accidentally extended beyond acceptable parameters.

> **Upgrade the firmware to the latest versions.** Vendors make changes that address problems as well as increase functionality. Make sure that you are of any vendor specific security issues.

> **Use strong passwords to access points.** Never leave the manufacturing default password because they are published on the internet and are well known. In addition to the password for accessing the access point parameters, make sure that the SNMP community strings have been changed from their default.

> **Enable WEP.** Use 104 bit WEP keys—even with 802.1x.

> **Use MAC address authentication, if possible.** Access lists can require significant administration especially with service implications of adding or removing devices and therefore is usually possible only in smaller facilities.

> **Change the WEP keys regularly.** Changing the WEP key every 10 minutes is recommended. Check with the vendor to see if there are management applications that can facilitate and coordinate dynamic key exchange.

> **Use a unique SSID and turn off the AP response and broadcast mode.** Verify that the access point has the ability to turn off response or broadcast of the SSID. Because the users are known by the administrator,

there is no security need to constantly advertise the access points but it is important for the administrator to know that RSSI (radio strength signal indicator) information is also broadcast as part of the message so if there is a lot of roaming between access points, performance will be slightly affected because clients will have to probe for available access points instead of already have the broadcasted information cached.

➢ **Use authorization, if possible IEEE 802.1x.** If available, 802.1x will provide a secure link from the client to access point by making sure that the client is authorized to connect to the access point. Authorization should be used in conjunction with authentication.

➢ **Use authentication.**

○ Compare the authentication method for support on the clients and integration into the NIC driver and APs for rekeying support.

○ For Microsoft clients, EAP-TLS is recommended because the certificates are already available. If your organization does not already support certificates, EAP-TTLS may be a better solution. Select a RADIUS server implementation that supports more than one method on the same network.

○ If there is an existing RADIUS server that does not support EAP (some older network authentication servers may not have support), this can be resolved by assuring that one exists on the network and then proxying from the older servers.

➢ **Use a Virtual Private LAN (VPN).** A VPN does not protect the physical layer of communication but adds an additional level of security by encrypting the data that is using the wireless LAN.

➢ **Use Static IP Addresses for Access Points.** DHCP is a convenient way to assign IP addresses but it makes it easier for an unauthorized user to install a rogue access point because it is likely that the network will detect two devices with the same IP address. Static IP addresses are just another roadblock that would need to be overcome for a potential intruder.

➢ **Disable "ad hoc" mode on clients.** By only having infrastructure mode enabled, clients must attach to an access point. This eliminates the ability for another wireless card (in an intruder's laptop) to create a ad hoc network and connect directly with one or more users. This may be more of a problem for corporate environments where critical information is store on laptops than data collection equipment that is using web services to access a remote application.

For home networks, the combination of a unique SSID, MAC Address Authentication, WEP 140 key encryption and making sure that correct firmware is installed with likely provide an acceptable level of wireless security.

performance. It is important that all installation instructions be used when the products are installed in these adverse environments.

Questions and Useful Tips

❖ *The spectrum analyzer shows interference across the entire band. How can wireless be used?*

➤ The first step is to understand what the interference is and try to address it. For example, a leaky microwave or microwave that needs adjustment may be causing interference problems in the 2.4 GHz band. It is much easier and usually more cost effective to replace a microwave oven than to move the entire wireless communication implementation to another band, such as 5 GHz. While 802.11a technology provides the technical solution, it is best to try to resolve the root cause of the problem before trying to avoid it.

❖ *What can be expected for wireless throughput?*

➤ In the past, wireless protocols had to work with limited wireless bandwidth as well as address issues that were not present in wired LAN architectures. Therefore the protocol used CDMA (collision sense multiple access) is more efficient. A rule of thumb for IEEE 802.11 radios is 50% of the raw data rate can be expected for data throughput.

❖ *Why is "transaction density" important?*

➤ It is important to understand transaction density to assure that there is not a performance issue with the wireless solution. If 80% of the transactions or packets sent occur in one or two access point cells, these cells are candidates for additional access points in order to provide more throughput for these areas so that clients are not waiting for air time to transmit their data. It is comparable to adding more lanes to the highway or road where the traffic is the heaviest.

❖ *Why is "peak performance" important?*

➤ Because it could change the wireless requirements. The wireless requirements are different if over an 8-hour day all the data is sent in the first hour and there is little traffic for the other seven hours, versus the same amount of data distributed evenly over eight hours. In the first scenario, there may be delays as all of the data is sent, which may cause frustration by the end user. Understanding where the peak transaction times are when the system is being used can allow the implementer to plan for this situation.

❖ *What is "IAPP"?*

➢ IAPP stands for Inter-Access Point Protocol. It is the communication process and messaging that access points use to communicate back and forth. The most important use of IAPP is for one access point to let the other know that a client is not associated with it, and for other access points to release the client so that multiple messages are not sent on the wired backbone for the same client. It is important to note that roaming and other inter-access point communications are not covered by the IEEE 802.11 standards and therefore this information is vendor specific until there is a standard covering IAPP. There are several proposals pending in various standards committees.

❖ *When should I use meshing?*

➢ Meshing should be considered only for a wireless infrastructure where the purpose of the wireless network is not portability. The issue of clients constantly moving from one place to another can introduce communication reliability issues which could negate the benefits of the wireless installation. Meshing could be considered for an office environment where the clients are in cubicles and do not move around. It would not be good for a data collection application where portability is part of the return on investment.

❖ *How can I prevent an intruder from getting access to a residential wireless LAN?*

➢ The two major weakness are the SSID, which is sometimes broadcast in the clear and not using the WEP key even if it is static. The first step is understanding the problem and only purchasing an access point that allows the SSID to be excluded from the Beacon and essentially hide itself from anyone that does not know the SSID. It is understood that changing the SSID from the factory default is a given. The only potential exposure that the network would then have is if the client needed to roam from one access point to another. In this case it would need to send an active probe and in this messaging expose the SSID but most *residential* wireless network have no need to roam because a single access point provide all of the coverage. Are there still ways to discover a single cell wireless network? Yes, but sending a probe request or spoofing a disassociate message through the wireless LAN in order to find additional information takes time and effort from intruder. The second step is to make sure that WEP is powered on.

❖ *What is the biggest issue associated with wireless security?*

➢ The single biggest issue associated with wireless security is that people and companies are not using any security. They are deploying wireless access points whether for their home, small office or remote office to get the benefit of mobility but are using the factory defaults which have no security enabled.

❖ *Can I use the defaults when setting up wireless security?*

➢ No. Windows XP, for example, is configured by default to log onto the first network that it sees, if this is a rogue wireless access point or another business's unsecured network instead of the company's secure network. An example of this scenario is a remote sales office where business may reside with common administration with a salesman using a wireless enabled laptop. Other possibilities include a retail strip mall or multi-story office building.

❖ *Do I need to worry about protocol filtering in the access points?*

➢ In order to maximize the throughput of the wireless network it is important that only those message that need to reach the mobile client use the wireless medium. Protocol filtering allows broadcast messages or messages not associated with the application running on the mobile clients to be filtered so that it does not use the wireless medium.

❖ *Why is it important to use static IP address for access points?*

➢ Using DHCP, while great for mobile clients, can cause numerous headaches for network administrators if they don't know that address of the access point. Without the IP address they would have to search each AP if there was a problem.

❖ *In general, what are the throughput expectations for wireless networks?*

➢ In general, the throughput of a wireless LAN should be expected to be ½ of the data rate of the radio.

❖ *Does a proprietary wireless network provide better security than the offerings of standard based solutions?*

➢ This question comes up a lot where companies feel that proprietary protocols used by vendors in non-standard wireless networks (either 900 MHz or 2.4 GHz) provide them better protection than open systems based standards security solutions. While it has been well documented the problems of wireless security, it should be noted that proprietary solutions offer little or no security other proprietary nature of the radio protocols. While these proprietary solutions will provide protection from "war drivers", people trying to attach to network through the documented security holes of wireless networks that have not applied the proper level of security or no security at all, they do not provide any protection from people that want to get on the network because these proprietary solutions provide neither authentication nor encryption once the proper PC card or serial radio is purchased with the correct radio.

Integrating Wireless Solutions into the Enterprise

Overview

Many wireless solutions do not need to participate in the enterprise. A single cell tool crib application can be implemented successfully and stand-alone. But many other applications, whether they are wireless access to email servers in office applications or inventory applications that are updating the enterprise resource planning (ERP) software, need access to many of the enterprise resources. Wireless is another layer of concern that rests upon a wired infrastructure that is complex to begin with, especially if it spans multiple buildings or locations. Wireless networks depend on a solid, well-designed wired infrastructure. Without this foundation, adding wireless can create a house of cards. Two types of enterprise issues affect wireless:

- Resolution of wired network issues for enterprises that have not been designed for the new dimension of mobility and
- System level policies that are used to manage the enterprise and all of the clients that use the resources.

Mobility versus Portability

These terms are often confused, but there are design constraints associated with the difference. Portability may allow the business to achieve its goals because users can access information throughout the facility. However, portability addresses only the physical issues of connectivity. Any device, such as a laptop, can be plugged into an Ethernet jack and then turned off, unplugged, moved and restarted; this is portability. Mobility, on the other hand, means that the device stays on and the network connections are maintained as a laptop or personal data assistant (PDA) moves from one location to another, either within a single facility or building-to-building. Not only are the physical barriers removed, but also movement throughout the network is seamless, regardless of whether or not the end users are moving across network segment boundaries.

BRIDGED NETWORK

Access points need to cooperate with each other to minimally provide roaming information as mobile clients move from one access point to another. With vendor specific wireless solutions, some or all of the packets on the wireless network have previously been and may still be non-IP or proprietary and categorized as "foreign" by wired based networking equipment and applications. Foreign packets were not a problem for bridged networks, which viewed the entire network as a single segment. This architecture worked fine in small, lightly—loaded, single application environments. To address the increased amount of traffic on the infrastructure, networking companies introduced routers to segment the traffic. A stand-alone, single segment or a bridged network is very conducive to use by wireless equipment because there are only endpoint boundaries. Roaming across hierarchical, routed networks introduces issues that need to be resolved.

ROUTED NETWORKS

For over a decade, routed networking has been the mainstay of wired architectures and the number of networked nodes continues to grow. By segmenting the wired network, routers provide scalability and performance benefits as the individual segments are shielded from the traffic on other segments. As routers govern traffic on their own segments, they primarily use TCP/IP to forward traffic from one segment that is intended for another subnet. This posed two problems for wireless solutions: the first was that vendor specific wireless traffic could not get beyond router boundaries, and the second was that mobile client roaming between multiple segment boundaries would lose their network connections when they roamed to a subnet different from their home subnet.

Instead of trying to swim upstream against the wired networking community, many wireless companies began to incorporate IP based messages as part of solutions, such as an IP broadcast for roaming messages and the option to use TCP/IP as a transport protocol. Today it is hard to imagine that the industry took this step. This change took time, and in some cases minimized the differentiations that wireless vendors had purported with their wireless architectures. As a result, vertical market data collection vendors dragged their feet. This nuance with vendor specific protocols posed a dilemma for some IT managers who were asked to turn on bridging for the routers, defeating the purpose of the router, in order to support vertical market wireless productivity solutions. Vertical market wireless vendors have continued to persist with vendor/application specific protocols. This slow to change attitude and the ratification of IEEE 802.11 cost pushed some wireless infrastructure vendors into adding value in other parts of the solution, as new manufacturers saw the market potential of wireless using the IEEE standard as a recipe for access point and PC card functionality and met the needs of the IT community.

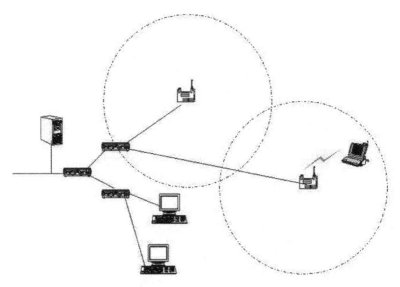

Tunneling

While the widespread acceptance and standardization on TCP/IP did not affect solutions targeted at office environments that were merely using wireless as a transport as they continued to use wired protocols, it did put many vertical market solution providers in a conundrum as customers refused to turn on bridging while they retooled their products to be IP-friendly. To resolve this issue, vendors quickly adopted IP-based protocols, which were not wireless-friendly because the size of the packet was ten times the packet size previously used for wireless communications. They also introduced solutions that allowed companies to bridge from installed proprietary protocol solutions to IP based solutions. One unique solution is tunneling proprietary messages through the standard IP based network, where messages bound outside of the current network segment are encapsulated in an IP wrapper and forwarded across router boundaries to known (and previously set up) wireless segments. Once the messages arrived, they were unencapsulated from their IP wrapper and placed on the local segment in the proprietary messaging format, where other vendor-specific access points picked them up. While this solution has wireless benefits, such as smaller packet sizes, it does include addition administration to set up the tunnels and has possible limitations associated with the number of tunnels that are available.

SWITCHED NETWORK

Instead of building a parallel-wired infrastructure or overlaying tunneling on top of the wired network to support wireless, a virtual LAN (VLAN) can be implemented that allows both to coexist. Virtual LANs use switches to logically divide their ports into multiple-layer networks. Access points can be placed on a separate VLAN from the existing wired equipment and the "wireless VLAN" can be given it own IP subnet. Packets leaving the switch going upstream are tagged with a VLAN number to keep them logically separated. Additionally, VLAN aware switches can be connected to each other and the tagged links can be used to join multiple physical locations into a single, logical network.

A VLAN implementation solves the problem for wireless vendors that have non-routable protocols because all of the segments containing access points can now be configured into a single IP subnet. This also solves the roaming problem because all tagged links are part of the same subnet. Tagged links can vary in cost and complexity because connecting multiple buildings may require fiber optic cable to avoid installation issues with long cable runs.

Mobile IP

If the mobile clients already have an IP address, there is another option to solving the roaming problem: Mobile IP. Mobile IP is an ITEF specification consisting of RFC 2003 (IP Encapsulation within IP), 2004 (Minimal Encapsulation within IP), 2005 (Applicability Statement for Mobile IP) and 2006 (The Definition of Managed Objects for IP mobility). Using Mobile IP, mobile clients are assigned an IP address called a "home location." On each Mobile IP subnet, there is a device that is the home agent containing an extra piece of software running transparently but keeping track of registered mobile clients for its home location. In early deployments and as an option today, the home agent can be located on a computer that is attached to the "home" subnet. Today, many access points can be configured to provide this functionality for wireless solutions, eliminating the need or requirement for another device.

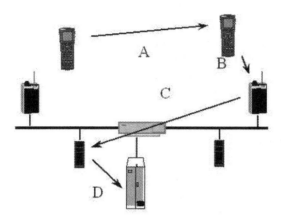

The "home agent" acts as a forwarding mailbox for the mobile client moving from its home subnet to a second subnet. If the second subnet has a Mobile IP agent, in this scenario called a "foreign" agent, it maintains the TCP/IP connection by letting the mobile client's home agent know where the mobile client is located. The mobile client, in effect, has two addresses. The home agent forwards traffic from the home address to the foreign agent on the second segment where the mobile client is attached and back to the home agent for as long as the mobile client is on the second segment. If the segment that the mobile client roams to does not have a foreign agent, the TCP/IP connection is disconnected. This same process works for any secondary subnet that supports Mobile IP and is not its home subnet. While providing a solution to the roaming issue in routed environments, it should be noted that a Mobile IP implementation does double the traffic on the wired to mobile clients outside their home location. For most wired infrastructures, the additional traffic adds little to the existing overhead.

ENTERPRISE WAN DESIGN

Enterprise wide area network issues deal more with performance of the network, including the wireless extension and how it relates to the expectations of the end user. Many times in data collection applications, the host computer is located in a different facility that is connected by frame relay, X.25, T-1 or T-3 wide area network connections. The total throughput of this connection depends on bandwidth that has been purchased but is typically less than the

Ethernet backbone or the IEEE 802.11 wireless solution. The key is to understand the limitations and set the right customer response. There have been scenarios where someone in the office at the remote facility is doing a database search on the host over the frame relay link and consuming much of the available bandwidth. The end users doing data collection cannot understand why the response time on their wireless mobile client is two-five seconds. One application is causing lost productivity for another. This aspect of system architecture should be reviewed as part of the overall wireless solution.

System Policies

Many companies have system level policies that allow order to be brought to managing an enterprise network. These system level policies typically include security, which has already been addressed, device management and network management. Integration of the wireless components while addressing wireless specific issues can make managing the wireless mobility an easier task in the enterprise environment.

Device Management

Enterprises worldwide are continuing to roll out wireless technology. The number of increasing devices has created dimensions and responsibilities of computing. With these new opportunities and benefits, wireless solutions come with their share of unique issues. Because IT administrators can no longer go to the server room or a cubicle to find corporate assets, device management policies must be modified. IT managers must plan and implement an intelligent strategy for wireless or risk significant downtime or loss of assets. It is essential for organizations to understand the differing needs in a wireless environment and implement a device management framework that will address the new problems and grow with the business.

Device management, in general, focuses on the collection of data and the distribution of data to networking and end user devices. These policies must now be extended to include wireless devices. In order to successfully accomplish this task, the implemented solution should keep a repository of all discovered and registered systems, as well as IT added components. This repository will also be able to collect and store device attributes such as serial number, available RAM and FLASH, elements controlled by revision such as operating system, application and drivers, and peripherals such as printers or scanners. An IDC study showed that fewer than 50% of companies actively practice asset management for their fixed IT assets, let alone their wireless components such as access points and mobile clients. The IDC study continues by noting that assets cost $120 per device per year to implement and maintain.

According to the Gartner Group, support costs alone for wireless mobile clients can account for 30% of the client cost annually. Despite the growth of wireless solutions, the installed environment remains largely unmanaged. Though, companies that attempt to implement wireless solutions without device management will experience higher operational costs and a reduction in the return on investment. The alternative is applying more IT staff to the task to track down wireless clients to bring them in for manual upgrades or put staff on ladders or forklifts to retrieve access points.

The goal of a device management solution is to promote network consistency, track changes, provide up to date visibility and lower the cost of ownership. The goals are accomplished by the following:

o   Tracking the device inventories
o   Support for rapid setup and deployment of device system elements
o   Providing a seamless distribution and monitoring mechanism for the following:
o   Data files
  o   Configuration files
  o   Applications
  o   Operating system and system components
o   Scheduled revision and update of system elements

Unfortunately, IT administrators cannot rely on the same desktop administration tools that are used to provide management and support of their connected users because of the nuances associated with wireless computing. There are quite a few of these nuances:

➢   While the access point may always be attached to the network, the client operates in a disconnected environment (which means it is not always there). Accommodations need to be made to address when the client is available.

➢   When the client is available, the bandwidth is typically limited and connections with a management system are only occasional. If a connection is lost or discontinued, the distribution needs to be resumed, not restarted, when the mobile client returns.

➢   Many of the clients in the infrastructure are not standard desktop operating systems, e.g., access points and environments requiring special clients performing different types of tasks not typically found in desktop maintenance, while clients may be using a version of Palm or Microsoft PocketPC or CE.net.

A Mobile Insights report, "Handhelds in the Enterprise," notes that wireless devices, and specifically handheld computers, can be successfully integrated into the enterprise system only if they are managed and supported as part of the overall IT enterprise solution. This presents a daunting task if one is forced to perform work manually, while physically touching the devices.

DEVICE COMMUNICATION

The most important part of wireless device management is what is being delivered to the device or from the device to the host or server, usually called the "package". The package may contain software, configurations, an operating system or application files. It may also contain a program or instructions for the device to gather information about the device that is needed by the host system. "Device" from a wireless perspective is meant to include access points, which are typically attached to the network, as well as wireless clients that are mobile. Once the contents of the package have been determined, the next step is distribution. The basic requirement for package distribution in a mobile environment is that it needs to be pushed or pulled by either the server or a user, depending on the situation, with or without end user intervention. Examples of a package pushed to wireless clients may include application software update or configuration change to a mobile client, new firmware updates to an access point or font changes for a printer. Information pulled by a server may include device application information that has been collected during work by the user. On the other side, information may be pulled by the wireless client for the onboard application when the user logs in and identifies them to the client application (or pushed when memory or other critical items reach predetermined thresholds).

Automated Detection of New/Updated Packages

While a manual process could include tracking down each device, providing the appropriate updates and creating a written log of changes, device management provides a reliable and less time consuming methodology. By automating the package deployment process, businesses don't need to touch devices for packages that may contain periodic software or firmware updates.

In addition to delivering the package, each device (client or access point) needs to be able to detect the presence of the package and needs to have the capability or understanding of whether the package needs to be opened immediately or at a scheduled future timeframe. This auto detection and time sensitive functionality allows a package to be prioritized in respect to the other operations of the device application. For example, while downloading a new operating system may take a portion of the communication bandwidth to load onto the device, it can disrupt work flow if it requires the user to log out of the application to allow the operating system to load. Additionally, if there are any problems, the user may be stranded for the remainder of the day (depending on the problem). If needed, the contents may be immediately opened and the variables will be available to the client operating system or application without additional intervention. An example of this may include change orders that need to be immediately processed by the application. Otherwise, opening the package could be time delayed to a specific time when applications are not scheduled to be running or a specific date to allow a variable window for the delivery of the package to the device. The time delay capability is nice to have for large populations because it allows all of the devices to be loaded and distribution problems to be resolved before all of the changes kick in. A good scenario would be loading all of the access points with a software upgrade that is not backward compatible due to new or changed functionality, if the package is opened immediately access points with the new program may not be communicate with ones that do not have the upgrade therefore taking down the entire network.

Packages Delivery Logging

As part of the administration frame for the device management schema, once the file has been delivered a log needs to be generated to confirm the delivery. This log needs to minimally reside on the device management server once the client has acknowledged delivery of the file. Optionally, the client may also keep a log for diagnostic purposes to know what it has received. The purpose of the log, on either side, is for auditing purposes so that the IT administrator can identify, through reporting, those devices that require additional attention because they did not respond to the automatic delivery process or did not successfully receive the package.

Package Errors and Reason Codes

The error process also needs to support the exchange of package delivery status codes. Error codes should be available at the server for reporting to indicate that delivery of packages was unsuccessful, along with a reason code describing the failure and action taken. Examples of errors could be file too large for storage capability of target device, unable to communicate with device after defined period of time, incomplete file transfer, or many others. Sometimes the answers to package delivery errors are simple, such as a target device is taken out of service. But other times, memory errors or internal problems may indicate that additional action may be needed. In reviewing commercial applications that provide this functionality, it is important that the IT administrator be able to use the experience of the device management development team as well as craft the implementation to address the scope of the business problems that need to be solved. For example, if the business problem is assuring 100% delivery of the package even with the added complexities of wireless added to the mix and the device management software does not have package confirmation or reporting, it is difficult to measure the intended metric without requiring that the IT staff "touch" each device, effectively defeating the purpose.

No Redundancy of Package Delivery

If the administrator attempts to push a package to a device that has already been applied, the device should send notification, such as an error message, to the server with the information. This prevents clogging of the communication transport with unnecessary packages. The server will have an override capability to force a package that the client feels is redundant to be received and applied. This may be necessary for diagnostic purposes. Again, the inability of the device management framework to accommodate this situation could cause incomplete downloads or overwrites of critical information.

SCRIPTING WRAPPERS

Scripting functionality adds another layer of functionality to device management. Scripting allows instructions to be sent in addition to the data. So not only will a data file or program be downloaded as part of a package, but the scripting will allow the IT administrator to identify where the files will be located and provide an implementation vehicle for the time delay functionality previously discussed. Once the package has been detected, scripting allows the installer the flexibility to specify value added operands, including moving of current files to safe locations and deletion of files once the installation has been completed.

Scripting Language Elements

The scripting language allows the installer to define what happens to the file once the package has been opened. The scripting language should provide the functionality similar to Visual Basic to provide scripting capability.

- Target File Location—This functionality allows the installer to define where on the mobile client the target files will be located.
- Warm Restart—A scripting wrapper on the client may request a warm restart to allow a new application or operating system to take effect. A warm restart resets the unit by enabling an interrupt, but is done without the intervention of the user. If the user has to intervene it is called a "cold" restart.
- File System Maintenance—This functionality allows the installer to search the device to find and create/copy/modify/delete targeted files as part of the scripting language. This allows the IT team to make sure that no other files have been introduced on the mobile client, and if there are foreign files that they can be erased through the file maintenance process in the scripting language.
- Remote Process Execution—This functionality allows the server to perform actions on the remote or mobile device.
- ReFLASH Utilities—This needs to allow the reFLASHing of this device and other internal devices, internal radios, for example. External devices that support external updates shall be included.
- Diagnostic Utilities—This needs to initiate a program on the device that provides information regarding the health and state of the device.
- Device Clock Sync—Set the clock on the device to server time. This function must support an offset to allow synchronization of clocks across a range of time zones.
- Automated File Version Registration—The scripting function shall supply the ability for each file downloaded to the remote device to register itself with an appropriate version number. This function must provide the option track with a specified list of files by assigned version number with each connection to the management server. The revisioning system is independent of the file being version controlled. This will allow the system to manage devices using third party software applications that have no knowledge of the management system or Intermec versioning methodology.
- Secure Remote Control of Device—This functionality allows the server to perform actions on the remote or mobile device in a secure environment.

While examples of the functions show why a feature may be needed, it is important that if a feature is desired it should be documented at the outset of the software evaluation for device management because not all commercial applications provide the noted level of functionality in this section.

PACKAGE DELIVERY SCHEDULING

The device management server needs the ability to schedule and allow the delivery of packages based on the time of day. This should be provided as a wrapper around the package that allows the script to run and be delivered at a particular time assuming synchronization of date and time with server and taking into account differing time zones for remote locations. When packages are delivered, it can be coordinated either for a single device or to a group of devices.

- Date/Time—Data can be moved on any date and at any time to a specific client, group, or multiple groups depending on the set up. This functionality allows time zones to be addressed as well as an entire remote location to receive the package as a group.
- Single Occurrence or Recurring—Delivery of packages can be done as a one time event or set up as recurring, allowing a period to be set for the recurrence. This should be by number of days, weekly, monthly, or annually. For example, instructions or data that need to be downloaded every work day to the user and while the package is delivered, or because the information in the package is subject to change.

PACKAGE DELIVERY PRIORITIZATION BY TRANSPORT

Packages that are sent by the client and the server need the capability to be prioritized based on the communication transport available. This allows business critical information contained in client data packages to be sent over expensive communication transports, such as WWAN, and to hold large files or non-critical messages until a higher speed transport is available. This is typically done with a query to the device. Packages should be able to be configured, to be confined to a specific communication transport or to a minimum transport cost for delivery to the client or the server. An example of this need is specifying that authentication updates needed for wireless connectivity can be sent only via secure wired Ethernet connections.

Encryption

Any communication should have an option of being encrypted using the security policies defined for the enterprise. This means that a secure communication capability needs to be established as part of the booting process because the unit may need to request a new operating or application to make the unit ready to use for the end user. If bootstrapping is done to load the application, it will be important that IEEE 802.1x or VPN capabilities be part of bootstrap in order to maintain the security integrity of the initial program load.

Checkpoint Restart

This functionality is the ability to resume failed file transfers or package delivery where they left off, should there be a communication disconnect, instead of having to start over again. This functionality is especially important for mobile clients that have limited bandwidth, such as an IEEE 802.11 2.4 GHz wireless solution operating at 1 Mbps in an area where there may be many tens of mobile clients in a single access point.

Communication optimizations should also allow moving only the changes from a file that have been previously transferred. Methods such as byte level differencing provide this capability. This functionality allows only the changes in a file to be sent to each mobile client instead of the entire file.

DISTRIBUTION OF PACKAGES

There are several distribution methodologies that need to be supported by the device management application. These distribution methodologies must support movement of management information in either or both directions. Also, multiples and combinations of files up and files down must be supported. An example would be a server that sends down five packages to a device and receives three from the device. The transport is assumed to be effective, and minimal "special" error checking will be required.

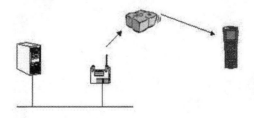

- One client—one package

A single package is targeted to a specific client. This may be a new data file or a new driver to be loaded on the mobile client.

- One client—many packages

A single client may need multiple defined packages from the server. This allows an operating system package to be delivered separately from an application update. Each may require different scripting to be implemented on the client devices.

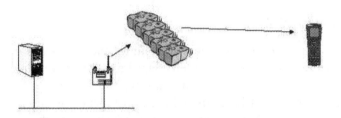

A client may also need multiple packages to define information that needs to be sent to separate applications or servers.

- Group (many clients)—one package

Groups allow the administrator to distribute a single package to multiple defined clients that have been grouped together.

- Group (many clients)—many packages

A defined group may need to receive multiple packages, such as an operating system and application update, which may require different scripting instructions.

- Multiple Groups

There should be no limit to the number of groups defined or the number of times a client is associated with a group.

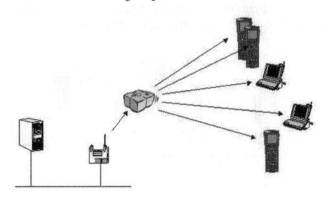

Initial Program Load

Each device should have the ability to boot to allow an initial program load (IPL) to occur, regardless of the condition of the Operating System or other software on the device. This IPL capability should be able to establish a security tunnel so that all future communications are secure. This should be the least possible amount of information a device needs to log in and obtain its software personality from the server. This IPL should be carried out over secure transports, making hijacking the devices as difficult as possible.

Device Management Asset Inventory

Before the package distribution process can be automated, it is important to know what devices are being used and what kind of applications they are running. Asset management software should be able to obtain a detailed configuration snapshot of each device including
- Last active date
- Hardware
  - Model number
  - Serial number
  - Hardware revision
    - Date of manufacture
- Device variables, e.g. total and available storage, RAM, etc.
  - Peripherals that may be attached
    - Model number
    - Serial number
    - Firmware/application revision
    - Date of manufacture
- Software version
- Application version
- Operating system version
- Independent system file version (needed for third party, non-participating software apps)

Work with the package distribution logic to determine which groups need which files, applications or upgrades via predefined rules. Detect unauthorized or accidental changes in the application running on the mobile client. This information should be stored and retained in a repository on the server for inventory and status reporting purposes.

Day to Day Management Policy

Day to day management is a process that understands where the wireless mobile computer is, who checked it out and when it was checked in. This has become an issue with the advent of industry standard wireless communication and industrial computers that look and feel like personal data assistants (PDA) with the operating systems, memory and capability to run non-business programs. It is also important to understand that traditional asset management programs were not designed for products that move around the facility and may have several people using the mobile client if the facility is running a multiple shift operations. Companies that deploy mobile client solutions including local area wireless, wide area wireless or dial up should have programs that have the follow capabilities. This checklist identifies functionality that can used to evaluate commercial programs or internally create a solution.

Equipment Check In/Out

Equipment check in and out should have alphanumeric fields that allow the company's employee ID, the manufacturer's serial number and descriptions of where the product is being used. This simple logging allows an equipment history report to be generated and a quick understanding of who checked out the equipment should it be missing in an inventory count. Additional reports can show all of the equipment used by an employee should there be an issue with damaged or failed equipment.

Add or Edit Equipment

This function is an inventory of all of the equipment at the site. The administrator can add equipment to the database, edit the status of the equipment (such as "service") or delete equipment that is no longer in service. The equipment information necessary for tracking consists of the following:
- Equipment name
- Equipment serial number
- Asset number
- Equipment type
- Status

The equipment name can be internally generated nomenclature that is used to describe the equipment. The equipment serial number allows for tracking by the vendor serial number. Some companies have their own asset tracking process and therefore methodology; the asset number field allows this to be included in the database. The equipment type can be used to differentiate different vendors or different types of equipment such as laptop computers, desktop computers, handheld computers, mobile printers, stationary printers or fork truck mounted computers. The status of the equipment can be available, check-out, warranty service, preventive maintenance, or out of service. The add or edit function should be password protected or allow changes to be made only by the administrator. This allows supervisors or end users to check in or check out their own equipment.

Batteries

It is important that batteries for mobile computers be listed separately from actual units. This allows the software to track the number of uses. One of the problems with mobile computers is that once the solution has been deployed, it becomes part of the company's business practices. Unfortunately, batteries are good only for so many recommended cycles. While some companies may elect to change batteries once a year, this level of tracking allows reporting of the number of cycles that the equipment (batteries) are used and therefore shows when they need to be replaced before the end users start to notice the decrease in battery performance.

Service

When equipment is sent to the vendor for repair or to have preventative maintenance performed, the equipment number and the employee number who sent the unit or who is performing preventative maintenance will be entered into the database. Both inputs will be verified to assure that they are valid and that the equipment can be checked out. The necessary inputs are as follows:

- Equipment ID
- Employee ID
- Date out (when checked out)
- Date in (when checked in)

This information allows service reports to be generated and gives information needed to follow up on equipment that is performing to less than the manufacturer's mean time between failures. Elimination of a single lemon will pay for the effort or the software necessary to track the asset information.

Add or Edit Employees

This function keeps track of all of the employees that are able to check out or check in equipment. The employee information necessary is as follows:

- Employee name
- Employee ID number
- Supervisor (optional)
- Work area (optional)
- Status

The Status field is the only non-explanatory field. Because it is important to keep all employees for historical information, the minimum values for the employee status field should be checked in, checked out and no longer an employee. The add or edit function should password protected or allow changes to be made only by the administrator. This allows supervisors or end users to check in or check out their own equipment.

CONFIGURATION MANAGEMENT

When left unprotected, configurations can too easily get changed on a per device basis or "messed up" in general. Configuration management should be able to centrally control network parameters, device information and formats, hardware parameters and application variables. The management server shall allow for the manipulation of the following device and infrastructure elements.

NETWORK PARAMETERS

Network parameters provide the capability of changing the IP address, DNS, DHCP server, security parameters, login parameters, radio settings or any other parameters that are needed for the client to communicate over the infrastructure. Single devices may have a multiple methods of communicating with the management server.

BEST PRACTICES

The variables for device management solutions are endless but the rewards for identifying and prioritizing the specific business parameters that are important for the application(s) that are being deployed will more than pay for the work invested. Best practices may include some or all of the parameters previously discussed. In order to create and take advantage of the benefits and whether device management is done through wired, wireless or multiple communication mediums, it is important document the goals of process.

Create a Baseline

Creating a standard process or baseline provides consistency and helps to reduce the complexity associated with wireless installation. Additionally it does three important things, it requires that the existing business practices be documented including the movement of data to and from the application and the device management needs be documented which will includes documenting information that is available and/or needed to resolve recognized issues. Documentation of the following data about the devices in conjunction with the select package delivery mechanism and/or equipment management practices:

- Baseline software versions including application, operating systems and driver
- IP addressing methodology and management
- Naming conventions including domain name systems (DNS) and Dynamic Host Configuration Protocol (DHCP).

Standardization or document of device nomenclature and the software will greatly assist in the implementation and setting up reports that will be device management process.

Validate, Audit and Review the Process

In addition to the normal operation of the device management process, continual testing of the process allows the variables that have been identified to be tested to insure that the metrics are being met as well as identifying boundary conditions. While initial documentation issued to create and implement the process, it is important that this be used as a baseline and occasionally audited to make sure that error codes and information returned through the device management system are enough to isolate any issues that arise. Device management and its implementation mechanisms provide a powerful arm that reaches through the expanses of wireless ether to remotely resolve issues affecting the end user.

Network Management

In today's world of information technology, network infrastructures and distributed processing systems have become critical with the emphasis on real time decisions based real time access. Within the enterprise, the trend is toward more complex networks supporting more applications and more users. While wireless networks have become a foundation building block for expanding the infrastructure, they are a small portion of the entire corporate picture. For network administrators, it is still important to utilize network management standards and framework and not make the characteristics of the wireless network proprietary. As these networks (wireless or wired) grow in scale, two facts become painfully evident:

- The network and its associated resources and distributed applications become indispensable to the organization.
- More things can go wrong, disabling the network or a portion of the network or degrading performance to an unacceptable level.

A complex network cannot be put together and managed by human effort alone. Historically, configuring the network was an art. As networked installations become more complex and more heterogeneous, the cost of network management rises even in the face of lower physical equipment costs. A recent survey found that an average of 15 percent of the total information systems budget is spent on network management. A network management system is a collection of tools for network monitoring and control that is integrated into the following senses:

- A single operator interface with a powerful, but user-friendly, set of commands for performing most or all network management tasks
- A minimal amount of separate equipment. That is, most of the hardware and software required for network management is incorporated into the existing user equipment.

A network management system consists of incremental hardware and software additions implemented among existing network components. The software used in accomplishing the network management tasks, the agents, which collect facts and figures, resides in the network access points (bridges) and communication processors. A network management system is designed to view the entire network as a unified architecture (wired and wireless), with addresses and labels assigned to each node and the specific attributes of each node and link known to the system. The active elements of the network provide regular feedback of status of each component.

The differentiation necessary for mobile network management is the need to drill down to the end node level, a requirement that is not a high priority for desktop focused network management solutions. The introduction of wireless networks has extended the reach of the mobile worker but has also added a new level of complexity for the network administrator. This complexity and reliance of corporate operations on wired and wireless networks requires the utilization of comprehensive management tools to manage, monitor and troubleshoot the network. The major goals of a network management system are as follows:

- ➤ Improve network availability (uptime) of the network
- ➤ Provide central control of network components
- ➤ Reduce the complexity of the solution as viewed by the administrator
- ➤ Reduce operational and maintenance costs.

While end node management and other defined requirements is a mandatory for mobile network management, it is not on the radar scope for enterprise network management companies that have expanded their solutions beyond operations management and into service management. This functionality may need to be provided by the a third party solution provider or the wireless vendor.

BENEFITS AND COST JUSTIFICATION

In addition to the features MIS departments are looking for in network management, the following is a list of principal driving forces justifying an investment in network management:

Controlling corporate strategic assets: Network and distributed computing resources are increasingly being added and need to be available to the entire organization. Without effective control, these resources do not provide the payback that corporate management requires. It is especially important to see if certain units are contributing at all if they are continually failing.

Controlling complexity: The continued growth in the number of network components, users, interfaces, protocols and vendors threatens management with loss of control over what is connected to the network and how network resources are used. This is why it is important to use industry standards and not develop a proprietary system.

Improving service: Users expect the same or improved service as the organization's information and computing resources grow and become distributed.

Balancing various needs: An organization's network information and computing resources must provide a spectrum of users with various applications at given levels of support, with specific requirements in the areas of performance, availability and security. The network manager must assign and control resources to balance these various needs. The network management system must be able to manage both the wireless and wired networks.

Reducing downtime: As an organization's network resources become important, minimum availability requirements approach 100 percent. In addition to proper redundant design, network management has an indispensable role to play in ensuring high availability.

Controlling Costs: Resource utilization must be monitored and controlled to enable essential user needs to be satisfied at a reasonable cost.

When looking at the software application, a functional breakdown of requirements has been outlined by the ISO (International Organization for Standardization) that is useful for the structure of the overall design. The ISO outline consists of fault management, accounting management, configuration management, performance and security management.

Autodiscovery

The most important aspect to network management for the application to know is that the wireless device exists. Therefore, it is imperative that it be discovered automatically. This will require that the wireless device generate the message to initiate the discovery.

Access Control through Autodiscovery

Access control to the network could be added where only devices that are authenticated through the autodiscovery process will have access to the network. This would provide an Intermec solution for issues such as rogue access points. It also would provide equivalent functionality to the Wavelink MobileManager product.

Grouping

This allows selected functions to be applied to a defined group of clients or infrastructure components. Performance measurements can be monitored by a group of access points or mobile clients rather than having to view the performance as a system function.

Device Naming Proxy

Devices can be named using alphanumeric strings that are attached to MAC addresses. Today, the only way to identify a specific device is the MAC address, which is difficult to read. This allows logical names to be attached to devices.

This is especially helpful for access points or mobile where the naming can identify where they are located.

Date/Time Synchronization

As with the device management solution, it is important that date and time synchronization be available. This functionality should be able to be implemented independently of the device management solution and is needed for performance statistics and other time sensitive information.

FAULT MANAGEMENT

Fault Management is responsible for detecting, isolating and controlling abnormal network behavior. Users expect fast and reliable problem resolution. Most end users will tolerate occasional outages. When these infrequency outages do occur, however, the user generally expects that he or she will receive immediate notification and that the problem will be corrected almost immediately. To provide this level of fault resolution requires very rapid and reliable fault detection and diagnostic management functions. The impact and duration can also be minimized by the use of redundant components and alternate communication routes, to give the network a degree of fault tolerance. Fault management functionality should include the following:

- The access point needs to send an alert that its physical transport has changed from wired to wireless.
- Host trace log to gateway; the ability to log to a file any messages being transmitted to and from the host of any gateway
- Docks need to send an alert if the client is engaged or is removed.
- Host trace log to direct connect mobile client
- Buffered view of LAN traffic; ability to monitor (trace) to a log file the transactions on any segment of the LAN
- Ability to determine the percentage of successful transmissions and retransmissions per each active device on the network
- Bit Error Rate Test (BERT)
    o Provide the capability to conduct a bi-directional BERT using selected communication paths
- Echo test—Ability to set up the system to continually poll and create traffic for a period of time that can be monitored (24 hours) to assure that connections are maintained, power is consistent and there is not time-specific interference. This is also good for installation testing

where cable connections can be tested to assure that there are no inter-mittent connections.

- The ability to set up a group of devices that communication can be automatically actively verified such as PING on a specified time inter-val. This would be useful in setting up a group of access points (APs) or APs and gateways that are PINGed at specified intervals which could be once an hour or once a day with a daily or on demand report.

ACCOUNTING MANAGEMENT

Accounting Management is responsible for collecting and processing data related to resource consumption in the network. The network manager needs to be able to specify the kinds of accounting information to be recorded at various nodes. This function is more useful under the performance management heading.

CONFIGURATION MANAGEMENT

Configuration Management is responsible for detecting and controlling the state of the network (for both logical and physical configuration). Start up and shutdown operations on a network are the specific responsibilities of configuration. There is also a need for the capability to initially identify the components that comprise the network and to define the desired connectivity of these components. The network manager needs to capability to change the connectivity of network components when the needs of the user's change.

Configuration needs to include the following:
- Current operation status of each active client
- Hierarchical structure of the network (spanning tree for wireless)
- Ability to ping any element of the network
- Ability to change a variable in the client or network component
- Ability to change a variable in multiple components of a group
- Ability to reset any node of the network
- Ability to take down and bring back up the network

Note:

This functionality should not be confused with the configuration aspect of device management. Device management configuration deals with download-ing a configuration file to the client independent of the contents. While there may be some overlay of capability, it is the intent of network management to be able to touch a specific variable of a client, as part of the troubleshooting needs of a network administrator.

PERFORMANCE MANAGEMENT

Performance Management is responsible for controlling and analyzing the throughput and error rate of the network. Network managers need performance statistics to assure maximum efficiency of the network. This is helpful in tracking the performance of the fastest path routing algorithm. Performance management should include the following functionality:

- Ability to graph the transaction times for a pinged message to a component
- Ability to graph transaction size distribution and specifically identify minimum, maximum and average message sizes for the LAN
- Ability to graph transaction time distribution and specifically identify minimum, maximum and average sizes for the LAN
- Ability to graph transaction time distribution and specifically identify minimum, maximum and average sizes for any segment of the LAN assuming one or more segments
- Network utilization percentages for each component in the network
- Percentage of transmission errors and type of errors for segment of the LAN
- Transmission and retransmission information for each wireless client and component
- Number of network management packets
- The number of packets specifically associated with the performance of the NMS function should be counted and stored to provide indication of the amount of overhead associated with NMS
- Radio Signal Strength Indicator (RSSI) for wireless
  o The ability to select a base and measure the RSSI to the terminals attached to the base.
- The following information should be kept by the terminals:
  o Battery data, e.g., number of times the unit has been in low battery
  o Ability to retrieve and view internal client diagnostics

SECURITY MANAGEMENT

Security Management is responsible for controlling access to network resources. Users want to know that the proper security policies are in force and effective and that the management of security facilities is itself secure. Information for security management should include the following:

- Log the number of times of remote modem attachment to each controller on the network

- Log and report the number of times a user accesses the network
- The ability to view and change security variables on mobile clients or infrastructure components

Drawing the Line: The Difference between Device Management and Network Management

It is important to understand the different roles within the system management structure. This understanding allows us to apply simple tests to functionality or questions concerning functionality to determine whether it pertains to network management or device management. The basic rule of thumb seems to be if you are doing it with a file in an offline manner it is device management; if you are working with variables on the client in real time, it is network management.

There are a few overlaying areas where the functionality necessary to accomplish the end task could be implemented either with network management or with device management. Configuration falls easily into that category. The baseline is that this functionality needs to be available to both packages as standalone entities; the major difference is the approach to the accomplishing the work. With device management, the configuration variables are modified on the Administration Console and placed in a package that is then distributed to the client, where it is opened and applied. Traditionally, this implementation best lends itself to be applied to groups of clients that need the same configuration.

With network management, the same configuration changes can be accomplished, but each device is touched individually through the SET commands of SNMP to the variables in each client. While smaller packages such as Wavelink Mobile Manager have blurred the line as they specifically address the wireless market for example with the ability to download profiles but enterprise packages whereas enterprise network management packages such as HP OpenView or IBM Tivoli would have deferred that functionality to a device management package.

Agents and Proxy Agent

Managing all devices whether they are SNMP enabled or not is part of the challenge of network management but is the goal of all network management solutions because without a total view of the wired and wireless network interpreting and resolving problems can be very difficult. As part of the up front design of a client or infrastructure component, it should be able to support an

SNMP agent and minimally be capable of being automatically discovered and provide MIB II information to the Administration Console. Different organizations including Product Support may require additional information for troubleshooting specific devices of the wireless network.

A wireless proxy agent (WPA) should be developed to support the network devices that lack the resources to maintain an individual SNMP agent. The WPA provides a common SNMP interface for collecting data from multiple resources at the same time, thus enabling the Administration Console to make a single call instead of multiple calls for information.

ADMINISTRATION CONSOLE

An administration console will be required to provide administration support. It will be an easy to see display that is designed to make it easy and intuitive for system administrators to use.

General Functionality

The following are general requirements are needed for development tools:
- Multiple level graphical map; this is needed for multiple building support but could also be used for multiple site support
- Must be able to export data to a printer or file
- ASN.1 MIB compiler for importing private MIBs
- Support for security so that the system cannot be access externally by non-authorized personnel
- Must be able to support at least two simultaneous network management sessions; this may be needed so that Product Support can access systems that have a dedicated network management system
- Must be able to support telecommunications to remote systems, e.g., modem support using PC Anywhere

UPSTREAM INTEGRATION

As noted in the overview, network management/system management application solutions while continuing to manage the operational aspects of the customers are moving in a different direction than the requirements needed to manage a mobile network.

USE SCENARIOS: USING WIRELESS NETWORK MANAGEMENT TOOLS TO TROUBLESHOOT

The purpose of this section is to identify several common issues with wireless networks and show how the tools that have been defined can be used to resolve the issues. The following are a few examples of how the tools that have been defined can be used to resolve issues in major trouble areas associated with wired and wireless network management.

Connectivity of Network Devices

Before any problem can be resolved, the device needs to be discovered or the troubleshooting methodology starts with the lack of network discovery and moves backwards. The availability of access point and mobile client discovery reports and screen updates allows basic issues such as duplicate IP addresses and other misconfiguration issues to be addressed.

The logical capability of information allows the administration to ascertain where the issue may lie with any component because the discovery process will proceed to three different levels. First, there will be a MAC address resolution, then an IP address resolution and finally the device name resolution. Failure to complete all three layers of the discovery process for the device will point to the level of the issue for further analysis.

Coverage Area

Coverage area issues can be assisted by the information provided by mobile client associations to access points as well as historical analysis of mobile client associations. A high mobile client count associated with an access point may point to a coverage area that may need an additional AP to handle the load. Questions can also be explored for access points that don't ever seem to have any mobile clients attached to them. Historical information on mobile client associated, either individually or as a group, could show that certain clients continue to leave the coverage area or could not locate an AP to associate.

Performance Bottlenecks

Network performance is probably the most important aspect of the mobile network management functionality. Graphs showing access point throughput, either individually or as a group, can be important to see if there is need for additional capacity in the network

Network Interference

RF channel packet counts for an access point provide detail information that may show interference. An excessive number of retries or significant spikes and valleys in the number of packets on individual channels could indicate issues that need to be investigated.

Questions and Useful Tips

❖ *Can I use only a bridged network to deploy wireless?*
  ➤ Generally, no. Most office solutions that use wireless as a transport from the wireless to the wired medium do not operate at the network, and therefore IP based computers and laptops are able to operate as they would if they were wired (provided that they have the correct IP and do not roam across subnet boundaries). It is important to understand that some data collection solutions continue to perpetuate wireless friendly, but use proprietary protocols that require all nodes be on the same segment or that bridging be turned on. In fact, using a bridging mode wireless solution in a wide area network (WAN) can be expensive if the company is paying by the packet or has to increase the bandwidth due to unnecessary wireless traffic.

❖ *How do I make my network management application wireless aware?*
  ➤ The first step is making sure that the IEEE 802.11 MIB is supported. If it is not, is should be supplied by the access point vendor. The IEEE 802.11 can be imported into the network management package.

Justifying A Wireless LAN: The ROI

Overview

In the past, companies invested in computers for the sake of the technology. Everyone assumed that computerized systems were always more efficient. But technology is only a tool, which needs to be used with a modified business practice that provides the end user with benefit (such as increased productivity). Increased productivity can be measured with several scenarios: the same amount of work with fewer workers, more work with same amount of workers, fewer steps to complete the task or increased accuracy (which reduces the number of times the task needs to be redone). The days of a free lunch for technology are over, as each capital expenditure now needs to be cost justified with a return on investment. It is also important to realize that not all benefits are tangible; some benefits cannot be measured, such as improved employee morale or more satisfied customers.

Doing a return on investment analysis is the first step to understanding the benefits that your business will reap using wireless technology. The report on wireless LANs paints a positive picture, reporting that the technology has an average return on investment of 8.9 months—with 92% claiming that they were able to ascertain "definite economic and business benefits" from wireless technology.

Selecting the Application

Selecting the application is one of the most important steps in presenting the business case to management or doing the return on investment for a project. Typically, there are many applications that can be wirelessly enabled. One of the issues is that many teams try to do them all at once and they lose perspective and focus. If wireless is part of a data collection solution, then the specific application needs to be identified. If this is an office application, the scope of the project needs to be defined. "Implementing wireless in the warehouse" or "Implementing wireless in the office" is not focused and convolutes the project and the goals it is trying to accomplish. It also hinders documenting the return on investment. The decisions that are made in this step will also help in managing the project as it moves forward. Failure to "draw a box" around the project can many times lead to a drawn-out, unfocused project that in the end does not accomplish the intended task.

DATA COLLECTION

Most companies have many potential applications for automating the data collection process. These applications can automate tasks (such as through the use of bar codes) to improve the flow of information to the workers from the current manual way or to allow information to be collected where it is better or easier for the worker. If this is a warehouse or distribution center, start with a single application or workflow such as receiving, shipping or inventory cycle counting that is communicating to an existing host; you could also consider a warehouse management system or enterprise resource planning (ERP) software package. These applications have been proven over time to provide an ROI, and industry associations such as the Warehouse Education Resource Center (WERC) can provide assistance in understanding the steps of automating these processes. Once you have had a successful implementation, the technology can be extended to other applications. Sometimes an integrated application requires a lot of cross-functional coordination within the company. It may be easier for a self-contained application (such as tool crib inventory management) or much harder if there is no automation in the facility. As the project begins, keeping it simple allows it to be broken into small, manageable pieces. These solutions are only suggestions where the road has already been paved; the uses of wireless for data collection are limitless.

EXTENSION OF THE WIRED LAN

When we are generically extending the wired LAN, it is more difficult to get a description around the project, and therefore the benefits, for an ROI. As with data collection, some projects (such as building-to-building bridging) are easily self-contained but the project needs to have specific, measurable metrics in order to be deemed successful. A general purpose solution of wirelessly enabling a department can lead to the entire floor, and then to multiple floors. While this part of the exercise is not etched in stone and can be modified, it is important to draw a line around what the goal is that will be accomplished by the implementation of the solution.

Scoping the Project

Once the application has been decided, the next step is to document the current workflow for the application. A step-by-step analysis of what is being done and how it is being done should be flowcharted. While this may be tedious, it will document for management what the current operation looks like and the improvements in the process re-engineering that will be used for cost justification.

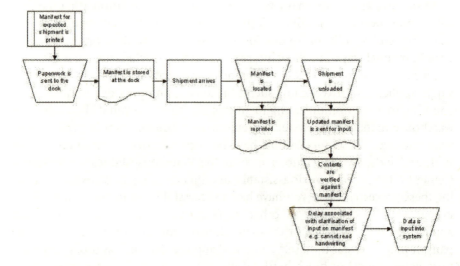

As the details of the process flow are documented, we can see why it is important to limit the scope of the implementation as well as where the improvements to the process can be made. Many projects will not require this level of detail such as a project to provide coverage to the carpet area of an office building for visiting employees to have access to the network. In this case, a description of the changes should be adequate to show the value and the cost justification.

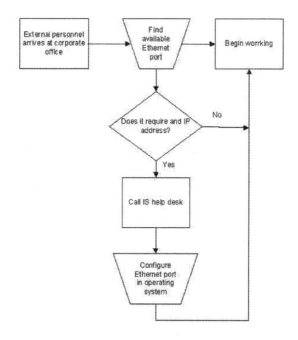

APPLICATION

If an upstream application is affected, we need to understand all of the steps that allow all previously enabled functionality to be completed. If, in the manual operation, someone entered data into an application, how will this data be entered in the automated process? Will this be a third party application (such as terminal emulation) or middleware where the input is transparent but merely completed by a different person? Or does this project require an internally or third party developed application which will need to be accounted for in the project costs?

SERVICE

Introducing new hardware or software means that there is a potential that it could fail or need support. How will service be handled? Service is an oft forgotten part of the project costs that needs to be considered, especially in a previously manual operation where there were no service costs. This needs to be integrated into the implementation costs of the project.

MANAGEMENT

Implementation of technology may allow for the resources to be better managed. The increased management methodology may be realized by the improved product capabilities. Whether it is software distribution to access points, configuration management allowing parameter changes for functionality or increased security, the ability to telnet or have web management access to the devices greatly simplifies the efforts that previously required that each device be touched by connecting a serial cable to make required changes.

INTANGIBLES

Intangible items are also called "soft" benefits. These are items that clearly affect the business operation but are hard to attach a specific dollar figure to for the business case. Increased productivity or general efficiency could allow additional orders to be shipped in the same timeframe, which may translate to more sales. Better inventory control could allow the company to ship additional orders because they know what is in inventory. Additional capacity for the IT team could lead to other IT projects completed that are helpful to other departments. In the end, more satisfied customers due to higher quality, faster response and improved accuracy can lead to additional revenue.

ISSUES TO CONSIDER

Independent of automating a business process, what's often overlooked in implementing technology is the "what" of the user experience rather than the "how" of the technical solution. Users want to make sure that the solution is ease of use, and management wants to be assured of ease of administration.

Ease of Use

If the process, typically data collection, that is being automated was previously manual, remember that users may be leveraging technology for the first time, whether they are blue collar or white collar. The application needs to be easy to use and tailored to the specific process that will be automated. Solutions that provide more steps or work for the end user may not be well accepted, even though they add value for the overall business. The value proposition for the company should be explained so that everyone understands the big picture. It is the same for an office implementation. Users should not have to worry about getting IP addresses or setting Mobile IP parameters.

Selecting the right technology for the right application is also very important, which means matching hardware to the application. If the solution is deployed in a warehouse, it should be expected that the hardware device will be dropped, and therefore a "drop specification" should be part of the decision process. Companies that install "commercial" or "office" grade products in industrial environments need to make sure that the service aspect of the product is adequately accounted for in the cost of the project. Because mobility also means that there is no power cord, another decision point is the battery life of the mobile client. Time spent by employees walking to where batteries are stored and changing them in the middle of a shift is lost productivity. The key for success is to get the users involved in the decision making process if there is a special purpose mobile client that will be used. Little nuances, such as buying a mobile client that has a full alphanumeric keyboard but is too wide to be held by the user, can signal big problems with the project implementation. Ergonomics is a big issue, especially in the Pacific Rim where the end users tend to have smaller hands than their US or European counterparts. All aspects of the project must be considered for a successful implementation, including buying a wireless enabled mobile client (if applicable for the project) that is suited for the end user and business process that is being automated. Buying the wrong or inappropriate device can lead to constant repairs, user frustration and poor return on investment.

EASE OF ADMINISTRATION

Wireless communications is only one of a number of new technologies that are being integrated into enterprise network architectures. Others include Gigabit Ethernet. Given limited IT resources, it is important that the introduction of wireless should not require proprietary hardware or software, including operating system and database technology, if applicable. Additionally, any client using wireless should be able to fit the network management strategy of the company. This includes software distribution and asset management. The addition of new tools for wireless specific functionality adds unneeded costs and complexity to the implementation.

Understand the Savings

The most common savings from automated data collection are labor costs associated with improved productivity, but a closer look at the situation is needed because material, operating expenses, inventory and fixed asset reduction can also contribute to the savings.

LABOR

When calculating labor savings, an important component is the variable cost of labor. The variable cost is the cash expense that varies in direct proportion to the hours worked. Do not include fixed burden, such as building rent or electricity or other overhead that will not be reduced if labor hours are cut. Variable costs generally include wages, payroll taxes and employee benefits.

For example, an automated receiving application is installed that will eliminate manual data entry of received goods. Currently, two people spend half of their time or 1,040 hours each per year (2,080 total) entering this information on a daily basis. A terminal emulation application on a wireless handheld computer completely eliminates this task. Assuming that the average earnings of these data entry clerks is $10.00 per hour plus taxes and benefits of 25%, the variable cost of this labor is $12.50 per hour. Total savings of this application is 2,080 X $12.50 or $26,000.

Using office automation as the example, the labor savings could be attributed to the time saved from having to address IT trouble tickets associated with getting remote personnel attached to the corporate network when they visit the corporate office, as well as the installation costs of the fixed ports needed for each visitor to physically attach to the network. This can be combined with the number of reorganizations or restructurings that require walls and people to be moved. While productivity deals with the people, accuracy is also a good cost savings—especially for data collection applications. For example, using a wireless data collection for receiving, put away, picking or shipping can be justified by the reduction of errors through the process flow. Typically, the cost of an error varies depending on whether it is found internally before the order is shipped or externally after the order is shipped. Each company has a different benchmark, but using $50 to correct an error as an example, if a company ships 180,000 orders per year and the automation solution assists in improving the correct shipments from 96% to 96.5%, this represents almost $50,000 in savings. Many companies will see one or two percentage points, which greatly reduces the payback timeframe for the project. Because of the cost per error, error reduction can be the single largest contributor to savings.

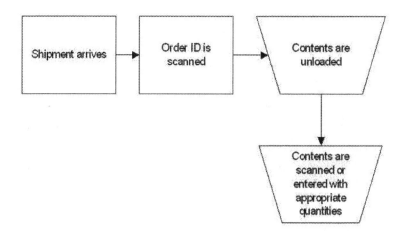

The additional components of this process flow are printing and maintaining the manifest and reprinting it if it is not found or is printed only when the shipment arrives. This means that a network connection and printer are required for this operation. If this is the only thing that they are used for, they may be able to be eliminated. If there are multiple printers, they may be able to be consolidated.

There are also intangibles for this process flow that cannot be quantified, such as better decision making because there is no delay in the arrival of shipments until the data is entered into the system or more sales because the ship date was better for the customer.

INVENTORY REDUCTION FOR DATA COLLECTION APPLICATIONS

Once the process flow has been documented, it is easier to calculate the direct and variable costs associated with changes in other aspects of the business. An important element for industrial applications and data collection in general is the ability to control the amount of inventory. Warehouse and distribution managers will agree that they could hold less inventory if they had quicker and more accurate information about the products that they have in stock at any given time.

The savings for inventory are calculated from a reduction in safety stock. If a company has $20 million in stock and currently has a 5% safety stock ($1 million) and is able to reduce that by half to 2.5% ($500K), it saves the company money in a number of ways.

Total inventory value		$20 million
Safety Stock	5%	$1 million
Safety stock reduction	2.5%	$500,000
Financing saving per year	15%	$50,000
Warehouse expense savings per year	5%	$25,000
Holding Costs per year	5%	$25,000
Total Savings per year		**$600,000**

ARE THE SAVINGS REAL?

If the application is justified based on labor savings, then it is crucial that it is explained what the company would do with the people that are affected by the automation. For instance, can the department reduce overtime or contract positions or get additional productivity? Can surplus employees be transferred to another department? Is normal turnover high enough that attrition will eliminate the overstaffing problem? Or will the company be faced with a layoff situation? Terminating employees should be a last resort. Not only is it expensive, but also it can be counterproductive. If end users fear that automation may replace them, there will be no cooperation. It is important that end users feel that the automation solution will enhance their working environment. It is important that these issues be addressed up front instead of at the end of the project or when the overall effectiveness of the project is being reviewed.

Estimate the Implementation Costs

The next step is to understand the cost associated with improved process flow. Start out with the project implementation costs, including purchased hardware and software. For data collection solutions, be sure to include spares, cables, batteries, accessories and service contracts. If there is work to the environment, such as bar coding locations or custom programming to the application so that the mobile client can use it, this also needs to be included in the implementation costs. For office applications, it is important to include any assumptions, such as computers, that need to be upgraded because the wireless drivers do not support the operating system or the hardware platform that is being used. Additionally, network equipment, cabling and adding power to appropriate locations identified in the site survey should be part of this step.

Even if the work is being done in-house, it is important to document what is being completed. For example, even if the facilities team will run the Ethernet cables and install the power, this work may or may not be part of the overall business plan (depending on how this type of expense is handled). Before the implementation can be productive, whether it is a process changing data collection application or a cable replacement office solution, the end users will need to be trained on any changes in the normal process. Even if the change is simply the assignation of a new wireless PC card for a laptop, a modification of the process for checking in and out from a central administrator or a new receiving and shipping procedure, this training must be addressed and documented. For larger projects, the company may use the vendor's services to do the installation, project management and training. Outsourcing steps allow personnel that have experience implementing the wireless solution while focusing internal resources on other priorities.

Hardware Costs	$150,000	
Hardware Spares Costs	$15,000	
Software Costs		
Purchased Software	$35,000	
Developed Software	$10,000	
Supplies and Miscellaneous	$500	
Annual Hardware Service	$8,250	
Annual Software Support	$4,500	
Installation Costs	$25,000	
Training Costs	$10,000	
Project Management	$15,000	
First Year Out of Pocket		$273,250

Hidden Costs

Beware of hidden costs of the project. This typically occurs when the process flow is not documented and the implementer gets to a part of the project and realizes that important things are not available or missing. Forgetting to do the operating system inventory analysis for driver compatibility can be a big "gotcha" when a surprise number of computers still need to be wired or upgraded/replaced because they cannot support wireless.

Financial Analysis

The financial analysis is the process of comparing the savings to the costs of the project. The income statement and the cash flow analysis provide the information necessary to calculate the different techniques that businesses use to determine the financial attractiveness of a project. Many businesses will use one of the following calculations to make their "go" or "no go" investment decisions:

➢   Return on Investment (ROI)
➢   Payback Period

Project Income Statement

The project income statement is the first step to putting together the information that has been gathered about the project and preparing the necessary financial information for the business case. Preparing each financial building block is beneficial, because it allows everyone to understand where the financial numbers are being sourced from so that changes can be made if necessary. There are a couple of variables that each company will need to provide the appropriate information associated with the project. In the case of the project income statement, you will need to know the depreciation period. While capital equipment may be up to five years, computer equipment tends to be three years because of the changes in technology. Additionally, there are multiple ways to depreciate the equipment. Per the assumptions, this example uses straight-line depreciation.

Year	1	2	3	Total
System Depreciation[1]	(70,000)	(70,000)	(70,000)	(210,000)
Service Contract [2]	(12,750)	(12,750)	(17,250)	(38,250)
Supplies	(500)	(500)	(500)	(1,500)
Installation Costs	(25,000)			(25,000)
Training	(10,000)			(10,000)
Project Management	(15,000)			(15,000)
Labor Savings	26,000	26,000	26,000	78,000
Inventory Savings	500,000	500,000	500,000	1,500,000
Pre-tax income	392,750	442,750	442,750	1,278,250
Income tax @34%	(133,535)	(150,535)	(150,535)	(434,605
Net Income	**259,215**	**292,215**	**292,215**	**843,645**

[1]   Straight line 3-year depreciation for computer equipment
[2]   Hardware and software service contracts

PROJECT CASH FLOW STATEMENT

The cash flow statement shows how the money will actually be spent for the project. The net cash flow, whether positive or negative, will be used for several of the financial calculations.

Year	0	1	2	3	Total
System Costs	(210,000)				(210,000)
Service Contract[1]		(12,750)	(12,750)	(12,750)	(38,250)
Supplies and Miscellaneous[1]		(500)	(500)	(500)	(1,500)
Installation/Training/ Project Management	(50,000)				(50,000)
Labor Savings		26,000	26,000	26,000	78,000
Inventory Savings		500,000	500,000	500,000	1,500,000
Pre-Tax Income	(273,250)	512,750	512,750	526,000	1,278,250
Income tax @ 34%		(92,905)	174,335	174,335	225,675
Net Cash Flow	(273,250)	419,845	687,085	700,335	511,338

[1]   The assumption is that service contracts and supplies are prepaid in the year prior to use. This is why there are no dollars in year 3 for this closed loop evaluation. If dollars are added to the previous year then the benefit needs to be added for the next year, in this case year 4.

RETURN ON INVESTMENT

Return on investment (ROI) is a key financial metric used to make business decisions about investments and expenditures. ROI is arguably the most popular metric used to compare the expenditures. The return on investment equals the present value of the accumulated net benefits (gross benefits minus ongoing costs) over a certain time period, divided by the initial costs. It is expressed as a percentage over time. In the case of technology, this timeframe is commonly three years because most technology is effectively obsolete beyond that timeframe. The equation for a three-year ROI is

(Average Project earning for 3-years)/(initial investment)

Using the example:

$$(\$511,338)/(\$210,000) *100 = 243\%$$

While the ROI tells management the percentage return the company will get over the specified period of time, it does not compare the magnitude of the investment with other investments.

PAYBACK PERIOD

The payback period provides an indication of the time it takes to recover the cash outlay for the project. The payback period is always express in a unit of time. In this case the period of time denoted is annual or per year.

Year	1	2	3	Total
Initial Cash Outlay	$273,2500			
Net Savings	$419,845	687,085	700,335	$1,807,265

The equation for the payback period is:

$$(\text{initial costs})/(\text{average annual benefit})$$

Using our example:

$$(\$273,250)/((419,845+687,085+700,335)/3) = .45 \text{ years}$$

With an ROI of less than 6 months, it is easy to see why applications such as the one described were funded.

Questions and Useful Tips

❖ *Why is walking through the process flow so important?*
  ➤ Walking through the process is important no matter how simple or complex the project may be because it helps everyone on the team understand what is being done and why changes are being made. It also assists in identifying benefits or intangibles. This step is especially important for team members from other departments who are contributing to the project.
❖ *What is the "target" return on investment?*
  ➤ The target ROI can vary from company to company and from project to project. Most data collection applications have a hurdle rate of 25%.

The Direction of Wireless Communications

Over the last ten to fifteen years, wireless technology has overcome significant hurdles—including issues of performance, cost and integration into the enterprise—to gain the mindshare of IT professionals as a viable communications method. As wireless becomes a mainstream technology for extending the wired network, it will face the challenges of new innovative uses. Radios will be embedded into everything, allowing almost any item to the capability of self-identifying or self-reporting. Things that we once thought of an inanimate, such as pallets in warehouses, will begin broadcasting where they are and their contents; tires on cars will tell the on-board computer about tire pressure or ID badges will not only identify the person wearing the badge but also be used to automatically log them in to workstations just based on proximity, such as policemen in squad cars or doctors at hospitals. Wireless technology will also be combined with other technologies to solve existing problems of which neither technology is currently capable. For example, when a cellular phone user moves from outside a building to inside the structure typically there is a loss of coverage if the phone automatically switches from GPRS or CDMA to a voice over IP routing. In addition to allowing calls to be received by continuing to provide coverage inside the building, the calls may also be billed at a lower rate than the wide area cellular communications. Also imagine a personal data assistant (PDA) that is configured only with an IEEE 802.11g radio, but receives email updates as the driver passes through a "hot spot" at a busy intersection. Or consider wireless combined with RFID technology that allows a retailer to tailor messages to wireless kiosks based on the identity supplied by the self-identifying loyalty card. The combinations and uses are only limited by our imagination.

Performance

Wireless has come a long way. Initial wireless solutions deployed bulky base stations and controllers connected to each other, while each client was polled through a broadcast message that was sent through a single base station at 1200 baud. Aloha and slot polling continued as coverage expanded with multiple base stations connected in a hub and spoke architecture, and the speed quadrupled to 4800 baud and then doubled again to 9600 in the late 1980's as commercial applications began to understand the value of mobility and porta- bility to collecting business data. Sending the changes to the clients and using multiple frequencies at a single site allowed the support of larger numbers of mobile clients. The commercial introduction of spread spectrum at 900 MHz boosted speeds initially to 60 kbps and saw wireless protocols make a slow move away from polling to collision sense multiple access with collision avoid- ance (CDMA/CA). Different proprietary implementations in the ISM band caused confusion for customers trying to decipher the bits and bytes presenta- tions by vendors. In the early 1990's, proprietary implementations ranged from 60 kbps to over 300 kbps as the industry also debated modulation schemes: frequency hopping versus direct sequence.

While IEEE standardization brought some semblance of organization to the wireless community, wireless did not catch hold beyond vertical markets until the 802.11b standard, which provided a wireless physical media imple- mentation that was comparable to 10 Mbps Ethernet with the high speed 11 Mbps standard. At the 11 Mbps threshold, IT managers can logically equate the wireless transport to a 10 Mbps Ethernet segment and the 54 Mbps capac- ity of IEEE 802.11g has knocked down the barrier completely. As technology continues to advance with engineers creating faster solutions, IT managers are looking to cost justify anything above the 11 Mbps standard unless the improvements are free and offer backward migration to the 11 Mbps baseline. This frame of thought can abstractly be compared to the movement in the IT industry of 10/100 Mbps Ethernet. While most Ethernet cards, in addition to the onboard chip sets integrated into computers, are 10/100 Mbps there has not been a rush to replace 10 Mbps segments unless a new segment was being added or the traffic on a specific segment (such as a backbone segment) required the change. In the same fashion, 11 Mbps users will not automatically jump to 54 Mbps of IEEE 802.11g without a business need, and as with 10 Mbps Ethernet, the market will require the backward compatibility to 11 Mbps performance, coverage and capability. Technology, though, will continue to move ahead, and developers will find ways of providing more performance from wireless waves.

Cost of Implementation

Another hurdle for wireless has been the cost of the implementation. Extending the wireless LAN was a huge cost impact for early adopters, with access points costing over $3000 and wireless cards having greater than a $500 price tag. This price impact made wireless a viable option only for vertical market solutions that could cost justify the hefty price tag. With the introduction of the IEEE 802.11 standard, costs have plummeted, giving rise to the horizontal marketplace. Access points and client enablement has dropped approximately 10 times. Some wireless PC card implementations are available for less than $50, which is now approaching the cost of Ethernet cards. And wireless is now a standard option with laptops as wireless is integrated into the motherboard next to the Ethernet connector.

Access points have moved in four directions as the market attempts to segment itself and maintain value add for niche solutions. Building to building communications provide additional software features that allow for traffic filtering or limited connectivity because they are not intended to support mobile clients but the focused application of point to point or point to multiple communication from one building to another. The second niche is outside coverage that requires an enclosure to protect the access point from the environment but where the access point still supports mobile clients. These special purpose units are used on docks and other locations that general-purpose access points do not function well. The third is single radio coverage area access points that are mounted in internet residential gateway. Typically these products don't support roaming other enterprise required functionality because the coverage is typically the home. Lastly is the industrial and carpeted space general purpose market for lack of a better description. This is the traditional market for extending the reach of the enterprise to the mobile worker. In all cases, the price of an IEEE 802.11 access point continues to decrease.

Integration into the Enterprise

After clearing the industry acceptance hurdles of performance and cost, IT managers are expanding beyond vertical market applications and into the mainstream horizontal uses of wireless. With limited staffing in IT departments, it has become clear that universal acceptance has at least one more hurdle to overcome: seamless integration into the enterprise infrastructure. IT managers need to be able to treat wireless as just another physical media that can be used with their network and system management applications along side Ethernet and other physical layers. IT managers are willing to integrate wireless to realize the benefits of wireless in the infrastructure, but not at the expense of requiring separate knowledge and tools on already overburdened staff and budgets.

Differentiation

With all of the standardization, the differentiation has been eliminated between vendors at the physical layer of the radio. Hence, vendors will begin swaying the pendulum from standards to proprietary by marketing "must have" features and functionality above and beyond the standards until the market decides on the most important features and the industry integrates them into standards. This functionality today ranges from wireless security to power saving extensions to self healing intelligent access points that can adjust their power and channel to assure maximized network performance or adjust for a coverage hole.

Next Steps

As wireless becomes just another physical layer that can be used to meet the mobility requirements of new business practices, the next big step is the multi-modal radio that integrates in-premise wireless (IEEE 802.11a,b, and g), which has primarily been used for carrying data with cellular or mobile wireless (GSM/GPRS/CDMA), which has been used with voice. Today the telecommunications industry has developed multi-modal radios that can allow mobile or cellular phones to be used around the world with a single headset. Indoor coverage, especially in large office buildings, continues to pose a problem as the structures interference with coverage. Once inside the door, the coverage seems to drop to almost nothing. While the industry attempted to expand mobile phone coverage with in-building antenna systems, the movement that will gain momentum and leverage is media sense seamless roaming from a cellular radio to a voice/data over IP 802.11 radio. This combination will provide ubiquitous coverage indoors, outdoors and around the world for mobile/cellular phones via in-premise wireless LAN for in building coverage, hot spots for public area coverage such as airports, hotels and high traffic areas and cellular coverage for everything else in between. Combine this radio functionality with the least cost routing software in the device, whether PDA or what used to be the cellular phone. And in addition to having seamless communication, the device will sense which mediums are available by evaluating the connectivity based on user set thresholds of signal strength and cost to provide the best seamless connection.

Small, First Steps

Many times we visualize technology taking large steps when it's deployed in new applications. Instead, it will take smaller steps that allow for incremental course corrections should they be needed along the way. In this manner, while we see the seamless roaming capability by mobile users as they change physical media within a single device and maintain session or connection persistence, there are smaller steps that must first be taken. Using the multi-modal cellular to 802.11 example, the first steps will be the integration of 802.11b radios in cellular form factors that will allow calls to either use cellular or wireless but not a combination of both in a single session. Threshold definitions and PBX integration as well as session hand off issues will need to be resolved before this functionality becomes mainstream. While these technologies will be used to address the primary phone functionality, integrated Bluetooth radios will expand the connectivity of PDAs and phones to a plethora of peripheral devices to add value for special purpose operations.

System Management Integrated Wireless Tools

Once a wireless solution is implemented, it must be managed and maintained so that the benefits and metrics can be documented. The industry has progressed to understand management. Both network and device understanding are needed for wireless devices, but the first steps have been third party add-ons to system management applications. As wireless communication is an extension of the wired LAN, system management needs to be ubiquitously integrated into enterprise level system management application and therefore policies. This functionality includes the following:

- Wireless devices, including access points, must be capable of being managed with the same device management and software distribution tools that are used for desktop or laptop applications to allow for operating system, application or parameter updates.
- Access points (AP) minimally need to be seen as two port wireless bridges or switches/routers, depending on the AP functionality and/or intelligence by network management applications.
- Network management of infrastructure components, such as access points, integrated into current system management applications need the extended ability to remotely address issues such as Quality of Service (QoS) and coverage without physically having to be on site.

- Security issues, such as authentication and authorization, will seamlessly integrate into the current security policy as well as address non-wired network issues such as rogue access points.

Virtual Site Survey Modeling

With the understanding of the theories and properties of radio waves as well as the general absorption of the waves by differing materials, the industry will be able to develop a virtual three dimensional (3-D) site survey tool by entering wall and ceiling dimensions, construction material and the other contents (current and potential) in the coverage area. The information could be augmented by testing data of access point placement and comparing receiver sensitivity to expected data versus actual. In addition to a site survey, this information provides a "site signature" because the information could be used to recognize any deviances outside a normal range and provide upstream feedback. With virtual modeling, the magic of wireless as a physical transmission medium will go away. Coverage holes that pop up in a wireless environment due to changing conditions (such as wall being moved, cubicles rearranged, racks or products being moved) will now be addressed automatically by access points working together in a self healing manner by adjusting the power levels to fill in where issues have arisen. Additionally, this information can be reported back to a virtual site survey tool that will update the site signature and perhaps generate questions that need to be investigated by the IT team to explain the new data received from the environment. In this case, the office or manufacturing environment has become a self-reporting entity.

WWAN and 802.11 convergence

The next step will be integrating the dissimilar physical media into a single unit. Today this can done by using PC card radios in different PC card slots of a PDA or laptop, but continued miniaturization of components (as well as middleware improvements) will soon allow communication devices to switch from GSM, GPRS or CDMA to voice over IP on a 802.11b/g with a seamless handshake on signal recognition and hand-off from the WWAN to an internal PBX.

Hot Spots, Multi-homing and Least Cost Routing

With the availability of general-purpose wireless coverage, today's hot spots provide an opening in the fabric of the internet, giving mobile users access to email and Personal Information Management (PIM) tools. Hot spots provide coverage at the "in-between" spots: that area in between home and work wireless networks. When additional access points provide increased coverage area to these temporary locations, users will spend more time in a coverage area before they roam to a new segment or a different physical media. If the period of time is more than a one time connect, issues such as multi-homing may need to be addressed at the MAC layer if they have not already been addressed through the use of a VPN, which is becoming more popular, at the network layer. Now that the industry is moving beyond wireless communication early adopters' end to end solutions need to implement least cost routing solutions to continue to drive down communication costs and encourage the use of wireless to extend the business proposition.

Intelligent Wireless Access Points

First there were base stations and transceivers. Then the industry moved to access points. And now fat access points and thin access points proliferate as the argument of distributed versus centralized functionality and computing power are extended from enterprise computing to wireless computing design architectures. Either way, both fat and thin access points will need to become "intelligent" access points. At the component level, both platforms have processors, memory, radios and network connectivity. The question is how much network value add functionality is located on the physical access point or in an upstream switch. The term "intelligent" is used in the content of "environment aware," so using inter-access point communication, access points will be able provide radio signal strength indicator (RSSI) information between themselves in order to boost or decrease power of their own access point platform to automatically assure that there are no theoretical coverage holes or roaming delays because a single client can hear five to eight different access points above its roaming threshold for good connection. This implementation does not require an upstream server to make these decisions. This intelligent subsystem will be able to boost power if it senses that an access point has failed, perhaps sending a proxy message to the network/system management application for further analysis because it has sensed a change in the wireless fabric.

Battery Powered Wireless Sensors

As the cost of radio technology goes down, it now becomes possible for it to be combined with other technology to make our lives better. Battery powered sensors could be combined with a wireless radio that provides only upstream communication to a central location, such as an access point. Because communication with the sensing device only requires occasional communication, the sensor radio would sleep for longer time periods and conserve energy.

New Applications and Technologies

As the technology changes, there are new and innovative ways that it can be used to solve business problems. Wireless networks are proliferating not only for data communication but also for collecting information in different ways and for different uses or for applications that we had not considered before but may be mandatory as our quality of life takes a step forward.

WIRELESS GEOLOCATION

Wireless geolocation is the ability to locate an item based on three access points being able to hear the radio transmission from the device. Using the signal strength information and knowing the location of the access points, software applications can provide information about the location of the radio in the coverage area. Today the issue is making sure that site surveys allow a device to be heard by three access points to be able to collect the minimum amount of information for the calculation. But the addition of controlling the transmit power of the access point can also be applied to the client, where upon receiving a signal from one access that this application functionality is being activated the client will increase the power output of its internal radio until it receives responses from three access points, thus allowing location to be calculated. Once the information has been gathered, the mobile client would reduce its power to normal levels that provide adequate communication with the enterprise infrastructure.

Medical Equipment Tracking

Today, medical equipment worth millions of dollars is moved from one room to another as needed by patients, but the continuing question concerns its location in the hospital. Usage and location data may now be collected by the same wireless infrastructure that is used for inventory management and patient point of care. Sensors attached to the medical equipment advertise the new information, which may also include maintenance requirements of the equipment depending on the type and usage. The key is that this is done on the same wireless network that is used for patient point of care. Imagine also an intelligent patient bed that uses battery operated sensors to identify care givers or equipment that is introduced in the coverage area of the patient bed.

Industrial Equipment Tracking

In an industrial environment where wireless coverage is already prevalent, the capability of tracking adds another layer to the available supply chain of information utilizing the same wireless infrastucture. Application data could be provided on the movement of everything in the supply chain from pallets to fork trucks. Sensors on equipment could provide diagnostic data on anything that existed in the wireless communication field.

INTEGRATED COMMUNICATION SYSTEMS

As size, performance and cost barriers continue to disappear, wireless will be used to allow groupings of items to communicate from a consolidation point. These groupings will be products that are not physically tied to one another such as items in your automobile or an airplane or ship where environment is large or that cannot be wired. This model could also apply to an intelligent home, where not only can the intelligent device communicate but also process commands over the internet or via a cellular phone.

Now that the technology is becoming commonplace, wireless radios will continue to be integrated into more and more, and with this integration the application will grow. This is just a small look at the potential of wireless. As the cost and performance metrics pass through the barrier of practicality, our imaginations for the use of technology will be never-ending. And the future is endless.

Glossary of Terms

10Base2	A cabling option for the IEEE 802.3 (Ethernet) standard. This 10 Mbps baseband over coaxial cable option has a maximum distance of 185 meters. Also called "thin Ethernet."
10Base5	A cabling option for the IEEE 802.3 (Ethernet) standard. A thick inflexible cable that is capable of transmitting signal a maximum distance of 500 meters. Also called "thick Ethernet" or affectionately called, "thick, yellow garden hose."
10BaseT	The current most popular cabling option for IEEE 802.3 (Ethernet) standard. This 10 Mbps baseband implementation uses twisted pair.
802.1X	The IEEE standard used in wireless security solutions that defines the operation of the MAC layer in order to provide port based network access control. Typically used to tie wireless clients to ports on access points.
802.11	The IEEE standard that specifies medium access and physical layer specifications for 1 and 2 Mbps wireless connectivity between wireless devices (fixed and mobile) and access points.
802.11a	A revision to the IEEE 802.11 standard that operates in the unlicensed 5 GHz band with data rates up to 54 Mbps.
802.11b	A revision of the IEEE 802.11 standard for direct sequence wireless LAN's that allows data rates up to 11 Mbps for 2.4 GHz.
802.11g	A revision of the IEEE 802.11 standard that applies that IEEE 802.11a modulation technique to 2.4GHz frequency range to achieve data rates up to 54 Mbps.
802.11i	An IEEE standard that focuses on enhancing the current 802.11 MAC to improve security

absorption	the process of wireless energy being taken in and not reflect by a material
access method	Refers to the way in which devices access the network. Traditionally used in terms of the connection to the network e.g. wireless, Ethernet or cable modem.
access point	Also known as AP. An access point is a wireless network device which bridges data from the wireless media to the wired media (Ethernet). This two port bridge device may also provide management statistics and additional networking functionality such as security authentication and roaming for the wireless clients that are attached to the wired enterprise network.
ad hoc network	A wireless network composed of stations without access points.
adjacent channel	A channel or frequency that directly on either side of the specified channel or frequency. In respect to wireless, channel 5 would be adjacent to channel 6 and due to the channel definition will have overlap which will affect the performance in both coverage areas.
AES	Acronym for Advanced Encryption Standard (AES). AES is part of the Federal Information Processing Standard (FIPS), which specifies a cryptographic algorithm for use by the US Government that is defined by Publication 197.
algorithm	Well defined rule or process for arriving at a solution to a problem.
amplifier	A device that is placed between the intentional radiator and the antenna to amplify the signal. In regards to wireless, an amplifier would increase the signal output and therefore potentially increasing the coverage area.
amplitude	The magnitude or strength of a varying waveform
ANSI	Acronym for American National Standards Institute. Voluntary organization composed of corporate, governmental and other members that coordinate standards-related activities. ANSI helps in developing domestic and international communications and networking standards. ANSI is a member of ISO.

antenna	A device for transmitting or receiving a radio frequency (RF). Antenna are usually for different uses depending on the application and different frequencies. For example, a omni-directional antenna for 2.45 GHz creates a 360 degree donut shaped coverage area tuned for signals in the 2.45 GHz range.
antenna gain	The measure of antenna performance, traditionally featuring an increase in coverage area, in respect to an isotropic radiator to which the antenna is attached.
application layer	The application layer is traditionally defined as layer 7 in the OSI reference model. This layer establishes communication with other users and provides services such as ftp (file transfer).
ASCII	Acronym for the American Standard Code for Information and Interchange. The 8 bit code for character representation is one of several ways to representation of data.
attenuation	The loss of digital signal energy where the signal is converted to heat instead of converted to the wireless medium.
authentication	The process a client uses to announce its identity to another station. IEEE 802.11 specifies two forms of authentication; open system and shared key, though most systems will other or additional authentication methods.
backbone	A term for a part of the network that is the primary path for traffic that has been transferred to the wired network from an access point. The traffic may be targeted to another access point or to a host application server.
bandwidth	Specifies the amount of the frequency spectrum that is usable for data transfer.
Basic Service Set (BSS)	A set of 802.11 compliant stations that operate as a wireless network.
baud rate	The number of pulses of a signal that occur in a second. A communications term that denotes the speed with which a digital signal pulse travels.

beamwidth	The width of the signal as it is transmitted from a directional antenna
BER	Acronym for bit error rate. It is used as a measure of the efficiency of the medium whether it is IEEE 802.11 (wireless) or IEEE 802.3 (Ethernet) and it is the ratio of bits that contain errors compared to the bits that do not contain errors.
best effort	It is best described as a priority of data across the entire communication medium (wireless and wired). Data that is sent via best effort means does not have any sensitivity to delays that may occur when higher priority data is encountered.
bit	The smallest amount of information that a computer can handled. Eight bits make a byte. The term is a contraction for binary digit.
BPSK	Acronym for binary phase shift keying. It is a frequency modulation technique used in wireless communication for 5 GHz IEEE 802.11a 6 and 9 Mbps data rates.
bridge	A network component that provides internetworking functionality at Layer 2 in the OSI model, the data link layer or MAC (medium access control).
broadcast	In networking terms, it is the dissemination of the data through the entire communication infrastructure without a specific target device. Broadcast message tend to be filtered out of wireless networks because they take up bandwidth without the knowledge of whether the data in the broadcast message will be used by any of the wireless devices.
byte	A combination of 8 bits into a computer unit of message. Bits to bytes, bytes create "words".
cat 5	Short for Category 5, "cat 5" twisted pair wire is cable that is used for communicating between Ethernet infrastructure stations that is certified for data rates up to 100 Mbps.
CDMA	Carrier Detect Multiple Access (CDMA) is the protocol algorithm used in IEEE 802.3 Ethernet.

certificate

A digitally signed statement from one company that typically verifies the identity or the content of a person or piece of software such as a driver. In the case of security access to a network, the certificate would verify the person requesting permission is who they say they are. As a driver, it verifies the identity of the company and thereby the safety of the software that is being installed on the device or computer.

channel

A wireless communications path that is described by a set of frequencies. For example, there are 11 channel assignment for direct sequence systems in the 2.4 GHz spectrum. Channel 1 has a center frequency of 2.412 GHz, channel 2 is 2.417 GHz, etc.

CKIP

Acronym for Cisco Key Integrity Protocol.

coaxial cable

There are many uses for coaxial cable. From a wireless standpoint, it is the type of cable used to connect access points to antennas. Coaxial cable is commonly called "coax" and consists of a center wire that is surrounded by a metal shielding or sheath and then covered with a plastic coding that may be color coded.

co-location

A wireless term used to describe multiple access points functioning in the same coverage area at the same time. In direct sequence wireless systems, up to three (3) access points can co-locate in the same physical area using the same total spectrum without collisions. In frequency hopping systems, the number of access points may be up to 12 before the number of collisions cause performance delays.

collision domain

It is the length of cable that signal can travel before communications timing from the protocol such as CDMA causes another device to place a message on the network and collide with the original message whereby causing a retry of the first message.

CSMA

Carrier Sense Multiple Access. A wireless LAN access method specified by the IEEE 802.11 specification

client

Also known as the end node, it is the device that is used by the end user to access the network.

data-link layer	This layer 2 of the OSI model transforms packets received from the Network Layer (layer 3) to they can be used by the Physical Layer (layer1). It also provides synchronization and transmission error control for the packets.
data encryption key	A string of alphanumeric characters that are used in conjunction with a encryption algorithm to scramble data.
dB	Acronym for decibel. A unit of measure expressing the logarithmic ratio of power, which may be a gained or lost between two devices.
dBi	A ratio of decibels to an isotropic antenna that is used to measure antenna gain
dBm	Acronym for decibels that are expressed as a ratio of power that is measured in milliwatts.
dBW	Similar to dBm except that the power reference is 1 W instead of 1 mW.
DES	Acronym for Data Encryption Standard cryptopgraphic alogorithm used by the US National Bureau of Standards. It is used in reference to wireless and wired security. Also see *3DES*.
device management	the practice of managing the configuration, software/firmware version and application parameters of end node devices in a wired or wireless network.
DHCP	Dynamic Host Configuration Protocol. A protocol used to automatically issue the IP addresses within a specific range on the network.
diffraction	the spreading or scattering of wave energy as it hits an uneven surface
domain	A general group of network segments or LANs based on common parameters such as organization, company, enterprise or geography.
DNS	Acronym for Domain Name Services. DNS is a network service that allows a literal name to be associated a network address. Typically DNS is used for naming servers.

DSSS

Direct Sequence Spread Spectrum. A spreading modulation technique approved for IEEE 802.11 wireless radios that uses a pushes the same data in parallel over an allocated spectrum of frequencies to avoid interference that may exist within the transmission band.

EAP

Acronym for Extensible Authentication Protocol. EAP is a mutual authentication protocol between the wireless client and a security server that resides on the network. EAP is used in conjunction with an authentication mechanism such as MD5 or TLS.

EAP-MD5 CHAP

Acronym for EAP Message Digest 5 Challenge Handshake Authentication Protocol. EAP-MD5 CHAP uses username and password within the EAP protocol to validate authentication to the required network resources which could be set up as the ability to connect to an access point or access to specific server on the network.

EAP-TLS

Acronym for EAP-Transport Layer Security. This authentication methodology uses a certificate or data encryption key within EAP. Certificates or keys are required on both the server and the client.

EAP-TTLS

Acronym for EAP-Tunnel Transport Layer Security. EAP-TTLS provides a similar security mechanism as EAP-TLS except that an encrypted tunnel is created before username and password are sent. This implementation is less processor intensive for mobile clients such as Personal Data Assistants (PDAs) while maintaining security.

EIRP

Acronym for effective isotropic radiated power. This is the a measurement of the performance of a wireless radiator as the power is released from the antenna. It is expressed in dBi where the "i" stands for isotropic.

elliptical antenna

A type of antenna that emits its energy in the shape of an ellipse to suit the coverage area where it is being installed

encryption

The process of making data unreadable by applying a key or algorithm so that it may be viewed or transported without being used or understood.

Ethernet	Also known as IEEE 802.3 standard. This medium access method uses CSMA to provides 10 Mbps transfer of data on a wired infra-structure.
ETSI	Acronym for European Telecommunication Standards Institute. It is an standards body that creates and proposes telecommunication standards for Europe.
Extended Service Set (ESS)	A collection of Basic Service Sets (BSS) tied together via a distribution system.
FCC	Acronym for Federal Communication Commission. It is the US government agency that supervises, licenses and controls the electronic and electromagnetic transmission standard which includes wireless communication.
FHSS	Acronym for frequency hopping spread spectrum. It is a method for sending data in which the transmitting and receiving systems hop along a repeatable pattern of frequencies in the designated spectrum transferring data on each hop.
FIPS	Acronym for Federal Information Processing Standard. Typically used in conjunction with FIPS 140-2, the US Secretary of Commerce has issued with the standard as part of the information Technology Management Reform Act with regards to data security for federal computer systems on wired and wireless networks.
fragmentation	It is the breaking up of a message into smaller pieces. In communication the maximum message size of one medium such as wireless is larger than that of most wired mediums such as Ethernet, therefore a wireless message would have to fragmented into two messages as it is transferred to the wired network.
frequency reuse	It is the ability to reuse the same frequency in the same time domain. For example, if two access points where located far enough apart such that they could not hear each other, both access points could communicate on the same frequency at the same time and not experience any interference.

gain

The process of focusing the energy of an antenna with the intent of increasing the coverage area

gateway

A network component that provides interconnectivity between disparate systems at the same or differing network layers.

Ghz

Acronym for Gigahertz.

hidden node

Occurs when two wireless clients cannot hear each other's transmissions typically because they are on opposite sides of the coverage area of an access point. This problem may be resolved by using the optional RTS/CTS which will resolve the problem but cause lower throughput due to additional required messages.

home agent

A mobile IP node specified in RFC 2002 that hosts the IP address for clients and establishes a tunnel for the transfer of messages to the foreign agent on the network segment where the mobile client is located.

hot spots

Nomenclature for one or more access points that form a coverage area in a public space typically for access to the internet.

IAPP

Acronym for inter-access point protocol. A protocol specification that describes the hand-off of mobile clients as they move from one access point to another as well as the protocol and other communication messages between access points because network communication between access points in not covered in the IEEE 802.11 standards.

IBSS

Acronym for Independent Basic Service Set. An IEEE 802.11 based wireless network that has infrastructure and has at least two wireless nodes or stations. Also see *ad hoc network*.

IEEE

Acronym for International Electrical and Electronic Engineers. A US standards organization participating in the development of standards for data transmission and communication systems

ISM bands

Acronym for Industrial, Scientific and Medical bands. The radio frequency bands that the FCC has authorized for wireless LANs usage. They are located approximately at 900 MHz, 2.4 GHz and 5.7 GHz.

interference	A term used for anything that disrupts the propagation of a wireless signal or causing errors to occur in the data.
ISO	Acronym for International Standards Organization. A standards organization working in conjunction with ETSI and IEEE to create international standards.
IPsec	Acronym for Internet Protocol Security that is a layer 3 security protocol option that is used in VPN devices.
kbps	Acronym for kilobytes per second. A network unit of measure used to measure throughput. With the advancement in wired and wireless networks it has been replaced with Mbps, megabytes per second.
LAN	Acronym for Local Area Network. A networking term for the collection of devices bound together for the purpose of passing information or sharing common services such as printing or file storage.
LEAP	Also known as EAP—Cisco, Lightweight Extensible Authentication Protocol is an IEEE 802.1x wireless security authentication methodology developed by Cisco.
link margin	This wireless term describes the absolute delta between the noise floor and the signal strength.
load balance	A networking term that describes the active monitoring of data through different paths on the network and distributing data evenly so there are no performance issues or backups on the network.
Mbps	Acronym for megabytes per second. It is a wired and wireless unit of measure associated with data throughput.
mobile IP	An IETF specification defined by RFC 2002 which provides a mechanism for wireless devices to freely roam from one access point to another though each access point is located on differing routed segments of the wired network.
mobility	A wireless term used to describe the ability to freely move a device or end node seamlessly throughout the coverage area.

modulation	A wireless term that describes the process in which electrical signals are transformed into waveforms that represent the same information.
multi-path	The composition of a signal with other signals from a transmitter caused by reflections which results in increased amplitude (upfade) of the signal or cancellation (downfade) of the signal.
near/far	Caused when wireless nodes in close proximity transmit a signal which "blinds" or overpowers the signal that is being attempted by a node that is farther away causing communication delays for nodes that are on the edge of the coverage area.
network layer	Part of the OSI model which provides routing information of data from the transmitter to the destination.
network management	The process of collecting and analyzing data from all wireless and wired nodes in order to protect and maintain the quality of service and throughput on the network.
omni-directional antenna	An antenna that uniformly transmits and receives energy from the antenna element similar to a doughnut.
OFDM	Acronym for orthogonal frequency division multiplexing. A modulation technique that splits the radio signal into various frequencies and sending the data on the different frequencies at the same time.
OSI	Acronym for Open Systems Interconnection reference model. It is a widely accepted architectural network model that breaks communication into 7 different layers; physical, data-link, networking, transport session presentation and application.
packet	A basic unit for communication of data across a network. Packet protocols are defined by the protocol standard such as Ethernet and contain source and destination address information, data and additional information needed to assure the packet reaches its destination.
PC card	Formerly known as PCMCIA which is an acronym for Personal Computer Memory Card International Association. It is a standard

set of physical interfaces attaching external devices to computers. It has traditionally been the form factor used for IEEE 802.11 wireless radios.

PEAP

Acronym for Protected EAP. A wireless networking protocol similar to EAP-TTLS except it was developed by Cisco, Microsoft and RSA.

peak transactions

A wireless networking load term which describes the total number of transactions over a small defined period of time such as per second. Previously wireless network load was defined over a 24 hour time-frame but in applications where 50% of the transaction occur in 5% of the time can cause unacceptable performance delays.

physical layer

Layer 1 of the OSI stack. The physical layer defines the electrical, mechanical and procedural specifications for the transmission and receipt of information bits.

pigtail

A term used for adapting one type of connectors (typically from an access point or wireless PC card) to another type of connector to attach to an antenna. It is not a recommended implementation due to the fragility of the pigtail, the exposure of the cables and the mod-ification of the connectors.

polarization

The orientation of the electric field of the antenna in reference to the ground e.g. horizontally or vertically polarized

PoE

Acronym for power over Ethernet. An implementation method that simplifies the installation of Ethernet by eliminating the need for power outlets at each of the end node. It is a method of injecting DC current over the unused pairs in Cat5 cable to provide the necessary end node power requirements.

presentation layer

Layer 6 of the OSI reference model. This layer provides translations between different data types to the application layer.

protocol

A formal description of a set of rules that govern how devices on a network exchange information.

QAM

Acronym for quadrature amplitude modulation. A modulation tech-nique that uses both amplitude and phase coding to transmit data.

QoS

Acronym for Quality of Service. QoS is the capability of network to provide better service including bandwidth or latency by prioritizing traffic based on the type of data or the application. Often mentioned in respect to Voice over IP were the ability to provide bandwidth is important in order to prevent jitter or noise.

QPSK

Acronym for Quadrature Phase Shift Keying. A modulation technique that changes digital signals into an RF signal using four phase states to code two digital bits.

RADIUS

Acronym for Remote Access Dial-In User Service. A network authentication protocol and service that is used by VPN and IEEE 802.1x in wireless solutions.

RC4

A security algorithm used by WEP (wired equivalent privacy) as defined in the IEEE 802.11 wireless standard. Considered to be a defeated algorithm after it was posted to the internet in 1994, it is not security when used for wireless communication.

roaming

A wireless networking term that describes a mobile client or end node as it moves from the coverage area of one access to another.

RSA

A public key cryptographic system named for the inventors of the technique; Rivest, Shamir and Adelman

RTS

Acronym for Request to Send. EIA/TIA-232 control signal used in wireless communication to request a data transmission from another device.

reflection

A term used to describe the change of direction of wireless energy when a radio wave intersects and bounces off another surface.

refraction

A term used to describe the change or direction of wireless energy as it moves from one medium to another. For example, when wireless energy changes as it passes through water or glass.

scattering

A term used to describe the random direction of wireless energy when it bounces off of a surface.

session layer

Layer 5 of the OSI reference model. This layer establishes, manages and terminates sessions between applications.

site survey

The methodology of mapping out where access points need to be placed so that mobile client moving maintain consistent signal strength with the access points. It can also be used to assure that the coverage allows for a minimum data transfer rate for example making sure that mobile clients in the coverage area can communicate 11 Mbps throughout the coverage area while roaming from one access point to another.

SKA

Acronym for Shared Key Authentication. It is the process specified by IEEE 802.11 where the access point demands a WEP key from an end node. This type of authentication assumes each station has received a secret shared key through a method other than the wireless network.

spectrum analyzer

An instrument that maps the amplitude of radio signals at various frequencies. A tool that is often used with site surveys or troubleshooting areas where there is interference.

spread spectrum

A technique used in transmitting and receiving radio signals that are distributed over a wide range of frequencies.

SSID

Acronym for service set identifier. The SSID allows for the logical separation of wireless LAN though all clients would be using the same frequencies for transferring data only those on similar SSIDs would be able to communicate to each other.

TKIP

Acronym for Temporal Key Integrity Protocol. A wireless security protocol that changes the WEP key after a predetermined amount of data is transmited.

throughput

The net amount of data transmitted minus the overhead associated with moving the traffic such as source and destination addresses as well as any retries required to get the data to the destination.

transaction density

A wireless networking term that describes the number of transactions that occur in a single coverage area. While the number of transactions for an entire wireless network may be low, there may be performance delays introduced if all of the transactions occur in a single coverage area.

transport layer
Layer 4 of the OSI reference model. This layer is responsible for the reliable moving of data from one point on the network to another including the ability to retry when data does not arrive properly.

U-NII
Acronym for Unlicensed National Information Infrastructure. It is used primarily in the US which is not part of the ISM band. Products using any one of the U-NII bands are required to have FCC certification.

VLAN
Acronym for virtual local area network. This is layer 2 functionality is not uniform by vendor but is functionality used in switch software to logically segment a network for isolation purposes. Similar to a wired version of the wireless SSID.

VPN
Acronym for virtual public network. Traditionally a layer 3 authentication and encryption mechanism between the end node and the VPN server. Though it operates at layer 3 and does not protect rogue devices from using the network, wired or wireless. It provides application and data protection on the network

VoIP
Acronym for Voice over IP. A technology that is defined by ITU-T specification H.323 that allows voice conversations to be placed into packets and transmitted over the data network along with data packets.

working path loss
A wireless term that describes the amount of left, which differs by frequency, after a radio signal travels 10 feet through a vaccum.

WEP
Acronym for Wired Equivalent Privacy. It is the optional security mechanism that is defined by the IEEE 802.11 standard. The implementation is currently being upgraded by the 802.11i committee due to issues, which allow the currently described WEP implementation to be cracked.

WLAN
Acronym for wireless local area network. A networking term that describes the combination of wired and wireless devices.

WPA   Acronym for Wi-Fi Protected Access. It is a subset of the Wi-Fi certi-
                       fication that deals with security. It is the industry group's attempt to
                       implement portions of the IEEE 802.11i standard where WPA 2.0 is
                       equivalent to the 802.11i standard.

APPENDIX A: SAMPLE SITE SURVEY REPORT

SITE SURVEY REPORT

For

Company Name
Location

Date

Prepared by
Name
Company

Administrative Information

Contact Information

Date Site Survey Performed
MM/DD/YYYY

Site Survey Performed for:
Company Name
Street Address
City, State Zip
Phone Number
Fax Number (if available)

Contact person
Phone Number
Email address

Site Survey Performed by:
Technician Name
Company
Street Address
City, State Zip
Phone Number
Email Address
Company Email Address

Scope of report

This wireless site survey is a process by which test data is collected and used to determine the appropriate location of hardware needed to achieve reliable RF (radio frequency) propagation throughout the requested areas of a facility.

The site survey report consists of the written recommendations of the site survey technician or systems engineer for the specified customer site.

Every effort has been made to insure that the proper type and amount of equipment is sold to our customers to meet the requested needs. An accurate site survey is a key component to ensure your RF system implementation is a successful one. We are so committed to this that we offer a guarantee.

The information contained in this document is to be used as a guideline for the mounting locations of the RF LAN equipment at the *customer* located in *city, state.*

SITE SURVEY GUARANTEE

If reliable RF coverage is not achieved after properly installing the RF LAN equipment as specified in this report, *site survey provider* will provide additional RF equipment as needed, to provide the RF coverage specified in this report, at no charge to the customer. If applicable, *site survey provider* will determine the additional equipment needed and where to install it.

This guarantee does not include any loss of coverage due to facility changes made after the Site Survey has been performed. This exclusion also includes any changes in the facility structure and/or layout, outside influences that may be introducing interference not present during the site survey or if the RF LAN equipment is not installed as directed.

EQUIPMENT USED

The test equipment used for this survey is comparable to the recommended equipment that is to be used at the facility. The test equipment consisted of the following items.

❖ *Wireless vendor* 11 Mbps, 2.4 GHz 802.11b access point
❖ Laptop with *wireless vendor* 11 Mbps, 2.4 GHz 802.11 PC card
❖ Two 7 dB elliptical antennas, utilizing a diversity configuration
❖ One patch antenna
❖ One yagi antenna

EXPECTED AREAS OF COVERAGE

After communication with the customer and/or site contacts the following coverage is expected:

❖ Complete indoor coverage of the facility including shipping/receiving dock including gravity flow racks. Also included is the additional outside storage located on the outer edge of the building.
❖ Coverage inside 15 foot trucks that will be opened and backed up to the dock doors
❖ Performance to be a minimum of 2 Mbps throughput.

SITE SURVEY RESULTS

SURVEYORS' NOTES

❖ There are no other wireless LANs or communication equipment in the facility that could cause interference.

❖ The site survey was conducted in the 2.4 GHz ISM band with the intent of using IEEE 802.11b radios.

❖ The site survey was done to provide enough overlapping coverage to allow continuous RF coverage in the event an access point should fail. Throughput in the area of failure could be reduced to as low as 2 Mbps, depending on the actual location of the RF user in relation to other functioning access points.

❖ It is expected that character based terminal emulation will be used throughput the facility. The possible reduced throughput due to a failure should not impact the performance of these devices.

❖ In the gravity flow racking, overlapping coverage allows continuous 11 Mbps throughput for operators in this area.

❖ The warehouse has smooth concrete flooring and an uncoated metal roof. The outer walls were insulated.

❖ For weather reasons it is recommended that the access points be mounted inside with the noted antenna positioning or the access point be mounted with an NEMA enclosure to protect it from the elements.

❖ The wired backbone is fiber optic with junction cabinets located throughout the warehouse, evenly spaced.

❖ Spare access points should be considered for back and/or expansion of the RF coverage area.

GENERAL ACCESS POINT MOUNTING REQUIREMENTS

Power and Network

➢ Two port power outlets and one LAN outlet within five feet of each Access Point mounting location (2 to 3 feet is preferred)

➢ If DC power over the CAT5 LAN cabling is to be utilized (Power over Ethernet), AC power must be located at each fiber network junction cabinet or each access point network hub location.

➢ See *AC POWER REQUIREMENTS* and *NETWORKING REQUIREMENTS AND SPECIFICATIONS* for more details.

Access Points

➤ Mounting brackets are typically available for each access point unless otherwise specified.

➤ A small 12" X 15" platform may be required if mounting brackets are not available or not purchased for the access point selected.

➤ If an universal power supply (UPS) [back up power in case of power failure] is used, an additional small platform able to hold the weight of the UPS will also be required at each power location.

➤ Mount all Access Points with the status LED's visible from the floor looking at the access point.

➤ Any special Access Point mounting requirements will be noted under *FIXED DEVICE LOCATIONS.*

ACCESS POINT LOCATION—AP1 (MAP COORDINATES L-10)

TECHNICAL REQUIREMENTS

AC POWER REQUIREMENTS

❖ AC wiring is to follow all local codes.
❖ There must be no connections made to high voltage lighting circuits.
❖ No devices prone to sudden surges in the power line or devices that contain electric motors should be used in the circuit.
❖ No single device drawing more than 20% of the rated value of the circuit should be used.
❖ Plan the AC power circuit to draw 1.0 Amps of AC power if no UPS is used or 2.5 Amps if an UPS is used.
❖ The preferred power source is a separate ground isolated power circuit for the RF devices.
❖ The power circuit, if possible, should be connected to the same UPS source as other networking equipment including the host application computer. (this will allow the entire system to continue operating in the event of a power outage and protect the system from power surges and brownouts).
❖ Thought should be given to how to power cycle the access points. In troubleshooting situations, resetting access points by power cycling the unit may be necessary. This can potentially be difficult because access points are typically installed in high places. A single breaker for all access points or a key switch at eye level can save considerable time and frustration.

NETWORKING REQUIREMENTS AND SPECIFICATIONS

Physical Connections
➤ The RF equipment at this site will be using Ethernet 10BaseT connections connecting to an Ethernet network.
➤ 10BaseT cable lengths must not exceed 365 feet without a repeater. A maximum of two repeaters may be used on a single cable run.
➤ For remote sites requiring WAN connectivity to a centralized host, WAN connectivity applicable specifications. An analysis of bandwidth needs must be conducted to assure that the RF system will have sufficient bandwidth over the WAN connect for proper (expected) performance.

IP Addressing
➤ An IP address will be needed for each access point.

➢   An IP address may be needed for each mobile device depending on the vendor selected.

Roaming Considerations

➢   This site will be switched with all access points on a single subnet therefore allowing proper roaming.

Wireless Security

➢   WEP 128 will be turned on.

➢   Open authentication will be used.

➢   Wireless security will be set up through customer's VPN. Clients will be loaded on each mobile client. There are no access points outside of the firewall.

FACILITY LAYOUT

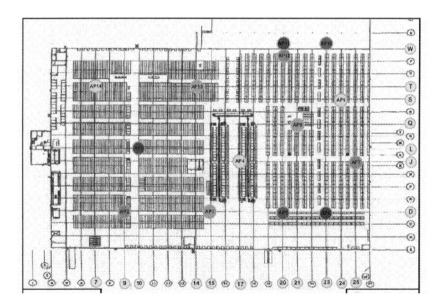

INDEX

0-595-32875-X